MATTHEW SARDON

You Are Not Alone
Christ's Presence in the Pain of Cancer

Copyright © 2025 by Matthew Sardon

All rights reserved. No part of this publication may be reproduced, stored or transmitted in any form or by any means, electronic, mechanical, photocopying, recording, scanning, or otherwise without written permission from the publisher. It is illegal to copy this book, post it to a website, or distribute it by any other means without permission.

Matthew Sardon asserts the moral right to be identified as the author of this work.

First edition

This book was professionally typeset on Reedsy.
Find out more at reedsy.com

For my Auntie Cristina —
whose courage taught me what faith looks like in the valley,
whose tears became prayers,
whose hope remained when strength faded,
and whose trust in Christ lit the way for all of us.
This book was born from your suffering,
and is offered in love to every heart that walks the road you walked.

"When you pass through the waters, I will be with you; and through the rivers, they shall not overwhelm you."

— Isaiah 43:2

Contents

Prologue   1

I GOD IN THE VALLEY

1 Fear Is Not Faith's Enemy   13
2 The God Who Weeps With Us   22
3 When We Ask "Why Me?"   31
4 Suffering Does Not Mean God Has Left   40
5 When Strength Falters, Something Sacred Begins   51

II WHEN THE BODY WEAKENS, THE HEART LEARNS TO PRAY

6 When Strength Fades, Prayer Begins   59
7 When God Feels Silent   66
8 Held Up by the Prayers of Others   74
9 The Long Nights: God in the Hours When Hope Feels Thin   81
10 When the Night Gives Way to the First Light of Hope   90

III HOPE THAT DOES NOT LIE

11 The Difference Between Optimism and Christian Hope   97

12	What Your Suffering Does Not Take Away	104
13	God's Power in Weakness	112
14	Nothing Is Wasted	120
15	Love Rising From Hope	129

IV LOVE IN THE MIDST OF CANCER

16	When Family Walks the Road With You	135
17	The Gift of Accepting Help	142
18	How Your Suffering Touches Others	150
19	Where Earthly Love Meets Eternal Hope	158

V THE STORY DOES NOT END HERE

20	The Resurrection and the Wounds That Shine	165
21	What Death Cannot Touch	173
22	Healing: In This Life and the Next	182

Epilogue	193
APPENDIX A — PRAYERS FOR STRENGTH	199
APPENDIX B — SCRIPTURES FOR THE DARK HOURS	204
APPENDIX C — STORIES OF HOPE FROM THE SAINTS	210
APPENDIX D — ST. PEREGRINE (Patron St. Of Cancer)	222
APPENDIX D — FINAL PRAYER OF SURRENDER & TRUST	227
About the Author	229

Prologue

There are moments in life that divide everything into a before and an after. A cancer diagnosis is one of them. It arrives without courtesy, without preparation, without the dignity of giving you time to brace yourself. One day life feels ordinary, even predictable; the next, a single sentence spoken in a doctor's office unravels the world you thought you understood. The air seems to thicken. The body feels foreign. The future slips out of your hands. You hear the doctor speak, but only a few words land with clarity: "We found something." "It is cancer." "We need to begin treatment."

A moment like that does not simply introduce a medical condition; it introduces a spiritual earthquake. It shakes the deepest places of the heart, the hidden places where fear sleeps until it is woken by a word that changes everything. Suddenly questions rise faster than answers can form: *Am I strong enough for this? What will happen to me? Where is God? Why now? Why me? What does this mean for my family?* These questions are not signs of weak faith. They are signs of being human. Scripture never condemns the trembling heart. The Psalms tremble. The prophets tremble. Even Christ trembles in Gethsemane. Fear is not failure; fear is the doorway through which God often enters.

Yet cancer presents a unique kind of fear. It is not simply the fear of illness, but the fear of vulnerability — the realization that your body, the vessel you have lived in your whole life, can suddenly turn fragile, unpredictable, unfamiliar. It is the fear of change, the fear of suffering, the fear that life will never again be what it was. And beneath all of these lies a quieter, more painful fear: *the fear of being alone.*

To suffer is to feel isolated. Even when friends gather, even when family surrounds you, even when doctors speak with extraordinary care, there is still a place inside the heart where no one else can stand. The fear grows there. The loneliness stretches there. The questions echo there. Cancer exposes this interior chamber more quickly and more honestly than most experiences in life. It shows us how deeply we long for Someone who can step into that private room of fear without breaking it, without rushing us, without asking us to pretend that everything is fine.

This book is written to speak into that chamber. It is written for the moment after the diagnosis, when the world feels unsteady, when the heart feels unprotected, when even prayer feels unfamiliar. It is written to help you see — slowly, gently, truthfully — that the loneliness you fear is not the final word. You are not abandoned. You are not forgotten. You are not unseen. Christ has already stepped into the room that feels too small for hope. He is already there, waiting not for your strength, but for your honesty.

Cancer often creates a second temptation alongside fear: the temptation to believe that God has withdrawn. Suffering does that. We instinctively interpret pain as absence. If God were near, we think, surely He would have prevented this. If He loved me, He would have spared me. If He heard my prayers, this diagnosis would never have come. These thoughts arise not because we reject God, but because we long so desperately for Him. Behind every "Where are You?" is the deeper truth: "I need You."

The Bible is filled with people who speak this way. Job cries out not because he doubts God, but because he cannot bear to lose Him.

Prologue

The psalmist shouts, "Why have You forgotten me?" not in rebellion, but in longing. Israel laments through centuries of trial, exile, and affliction because her covenant with God is the very thing she refuses to surrender. The cry of the suffering believer is not unbelief — it is love refusing to let go.

And then comes the most astonishing truth of all: God does not rebuke this cry. He receives it. He enters it. He makes it His own. When Jesus kneels in Gethsemane, trembling under the weight of what is coming, He does not speak with distant serenity. He prays with a heart laid bare. He falls to the ground. He sweats blood. He asks the Father if the cup can pass. And when it does not, He does not run. He does not deny His fear. He places His fear into the Father's hands. "Not My will, but Yours be done." This is not resignation. It is trust at the edge of human endurance.

And when He hangs upon the Cross, the Son of God speaks the words every suffering believer has felt: "My God, My God, why have You forsaken Me?" This is not a collapse of faith. It is the perfect expression of faith — not a faith that sees, but a faith that clings. Jesus prays the darkest words of Scripture so that no one who prays them is ever truly alone. He descends into the depths of human pain, not to observe it, but to inhabit it.

This means something extraordinary for every person walking through cancer:

There is no fear you can feel that Christ has not already entered.

There is no loneliness you face that Christ has not already filled with His presence.

There is no suffering you endure that Christ has not already carried — not to remove it instantly, but to carry it with you.

Christ does not watch your suffering from a distance the way others might watch a storm from the safety of a warm house. He steps into the storm. He stands beside you in winds that threaten to break you. His love does not prevent the storm, but His presence changes its meaning.

This book does not claim to answer every question cancer raises. No human book could. It does not claim that suffering is simple, or that faith removes pain, or that prayer always calms the storm immediately. It does not offer easy assurances or tidy explanations. Cancer is too heavy for clichés, too real for sentimental optimism.

What this book offers instead is companionship — the companionship of Christ, who walks every step of this path before you walk it, within you as you walk it, and after you feel you cannot walk any further. It offers a way of seeing your suffering that does not erase the pain, but reveals the presence of God within it. It offers reassurance that the tears you shed are not unnoticed, the fear you feel is not despised, the questions you ask are not rejected.

This book will speak of how to pray when words feel impossible.

How to trust when trust feels fragile.

How to rest when the nights are long.

How to find meaning when the heart feels empty.

How to hope when the future feels uncertain.

How to see Christ not in spite of your suffering, but within it.

You may not feel strong right now. You may not feel brave. You may not feel prepared for what lies ahead. That is alright. God does not ask for strength you do not have. He does not ask for a courage you cannot feel. He does not ask you to pretend.

He asks only that you let Him be near.

If you can take one small breath and say, "Be with me," that is already a prayer that reaches the heart of God. If you can speak His name in a whisper, that whisper becomes the cry of a soul held firmly in His hands. If you cannot pray at all, if the fear feels too heavy for words, then Christ prays within you. The Spirit prays for you with groanings deeper than speech, deeper than thought, deeper than the fear that trembles inside you.

Prologue

You are not alone. You have never been alone. The One who formed your body, who knows every cell, every hair, every breath, is closer to you now than you have ever imagined. He accompanies you not as an observer, but as the God who carries His people through the valley of the shadow of death — not around it, not above it, but through it.

This is the heart of the book you now hold. It is an invitation to walk with Christ through the mystery of suffering, to discover that even in the darkest valley, the path is not empty. It is lined with the footprints of the One who walked it first. It is illuminated by a presence that does not always remove the darkness but refuses to let the darkness have the final word.

There will be days when the diagnosis feels heavier than your strength. Days when the treatment drains more than the cancer itself. Days when you wake and feel a weight in your chest before you speak a single word. Days when the mirror reflects a face that feels unfamiliar — thinner, weaker, more tired, marked by the battle you did not choose but must now fight.

On those days, it is easy to believe that God is far away. Pain has a way of shrinking the world until all you can see is the present moment, the present fear, the present weakness. It becomes difficult to remember anything beyond the immediate struggle. Hope feels like an idea for other people, not for you. Joy feels inaccessible. Strength feels like a distant memory.

But this is precisely where the gospel speaks its quietest, strongest word: Christ remains.

Not because you feel Him.

Not because you understand Him.

Not because you are praying perfectly or believing heroically.

He remains because His love does not depend on your strength. It depends on His. And His strength does not waver.

Scripture never presents God's love as something fragile or conditional. The love of God is not a candle that flickers in the wind of suffering. It is the sun — steady, constant, burning even when clouds hide it from sight. You do not have to feel the warmth for it to be real. You do not have to see the horizon for the light to be rising. You do not have to understand the path for the Shepherd to be guiding your steps.

The pages of this book will walk with you through different dimensions of this experience: the fear, the loneliness, the spiritual dryness, the search for meaning, the difficult questions, the hope that can survive even the heaviest sorrow. But the foundation beneath every chapter is the same truth spoken from the heart of Christ: "I am with you always."

Not "I am with you when you are strong."

Not "I am with you when you understand."

Not "I am with you when you feel Me."

Always.

Cancer does not nullify that promise. If anything, it reveals its depth. God's presence is not proven by ease or comfort. It is proven by faithfulness in the midst of suffering. A God who remained on the Cross does not abandon those who face the smaller crosses that life places upon our shoulders. A God who walked into death does not fear the valleys where His children now walk. A God who rose from the grave does not allow any darkness to have the last word over those who belong to Him.

This means that your suffering — as heavy, frightening, and exhausting as it is — is not meaningless. Christ has entered it. Christ walks within it. Christ works through it. You may not yet see how; few do when they are in the midst of the storm. But the presence of Christ is not measured by your vision. It is measured by His fidelity. And His fidelity is absolute.

There will be moments in this journey when you look around and see signs of God's care: a friend who arrives at the perfect moment, a doctor whose wisdom steadies your fear, a family member whose embrace feels like strength, a peace that comes unexpectedly, a courage that rises quietly when you thought you had none left. These are not coincidences. They are threads of grace woven into the fabric of your days. They do not erase the suffering, but they reveal that suffering is not the whole story.

Other moments will offer no such clarity. You will sit in waiting rooms under fluorescent lights that make everything feel colder than it is. You will wait for phone calls that determine next steps. You will hear numbers, measurements, scan results, words that sound clinical but carry the weight of hope and fear together. In those moments, grace may feel invisible — but invisibility is not absence. The deepest work God does in the soul is often done in silence. The strongest bonds He forms are often forged in darkness.

Cancer forces you to ask questions you never imagined asking. It confronts you with limits you did not want to meet. It reveals the vulnerability of the human body. But it can also reveal the invincibility of God's love. It can open the heart to prayer in new ways. It can deepen compassion, awaken gratitude, purify priorities, and uncover strengths you did not know you possessed. None of this romanticizes suffering. It simply recognizes that God never wastes the wounds He allows His children to bear.

The saints often speak of this mysterious truth. Not because their suffering was less intense, but because they discovered Someone in the midst of it. St. Paul carried afflictions that would break most men, yet he wrote with unshakable confidence: "When I am weak, then I am strong." St. Thérèse endured illness with a heart that clung to Christ even when consolation disappeared. St. John Paul II, who walked through cancer himself, insisted that the human person discovers his true dignity not in strength, but in fidelity — fidelity to God, and fidelity to love.

Their witness matters because it tells you something essential:

The presence of suffering does not mean the absence of God.

The presence of Christ does not mean the absence of suffering.

The two can coexist. They often do. And it is in their coexistence that holiness, courage, and peace begin to take shape in the soul.

This book is not written to rush you through your pain. It is written to accompany you. To sit with you. To hold vigil with you the way the Church stands at the foot of every cross her children bear. It is written to help you breathe again when the weight feels heavy, to help you lift your eyes when the horizon seems dim, to help you trust that Christ is nearer than the heartbeat you carry through each long night.

In time, perhaps sooner than you expect, you may discover moments of quiet grace — small resurrections — in the middle of your journey. They will not erase what is difficult, but they will remind you that difficult does not mean hopeless. You may discover that you are braver than you knew, stronger than you feared, more loved than you imagined. You may come to see that even here, in the place you never wanted to be, God is writing a story — not of defeat, but of fidelity; not of abandonment, but of accompaniment; not of despair, but of a hope that is tested and therefore becomes unbreakable.

Let this be the truth that carries you as you turn the page:

Nothing you face will be faced alone.

Not a single appointment.

Not a single night.

Not a single fear.

Not a single tear.

Christ walks with you.

Christ remains with you.

Christ suffers with you.

Christ strengthens you.

Prologue

Christ loves you through every breath, every moment, every step.

If this book accomplishes anything, let it be this: that you feel, in the depths of your soul, the truth that Christ Himself speaks over you — a truth stronger than cancer, stronger than fear, stronger than death itself:

"You are not alone."

I

GOD IN THE VALLEY

One

Fear Is Not Faith's Enemy

Fear enters quickly after a diagnosis. It does not knock, or wait politely, or give you time to gather yourself. It comes like a tide, filling the mind, tightening the chest, unsettling even the strongest person. You can be sitting in a doctor's office one minute and find your whole inner world shaking the next. A single sentence changes the shape of your thoughts. A single scan shifts the horizon of everything familiar. You hear the doctor's voice, you watch their face, and something deep within you tries to understand what this news means for your life, your relationships, your future. Fear, in that moment, is not a sign of weakness. It is the natural response of a heart that suddenly realizes how fragile the world can be.

People sometimes speak as though faith should shield us from this. As if belief in God should produce an unshakeable calm, a serenity that nothing can disturb. You may even feel the temptation to blame yourself for being afraid, imagining that a stronger Christian would face cancer with perfect composure. Yet Scripture never asks for this kind of stoicism. God never rebukes a trembling heart. The Psalms tremble. The prophets tremble. Even the apostles tremble. And Christ Himself, the Son of God, trembles in Gethsemane. His hands shook. His knees bent. His soul grew sorrowful to the point of death. If fear were proof of weak faith, the Gospels would present a very different story. Instead, they show us a Saviour who does not deny His fear but brings it into the presence of the Father.

This means something liberating: fear is not the opposite of faith. Fear is the doorway through which faith must often pass. Faith is not the absence of fear; it is the decision to trust God in the midst of fear. A person without fear does not need trust. Only the trembling heart has the opportunity to place itself fully into God's hands.

Cancer introduces a fear that reaches places other fears do not. It touches the body, the imagination, the future. It awakens questions you did not expect to face: What will happen to me? Am I strong enough for this? What will treatment be like? How will my family cope? Why is this happening now? These questions rise quickly, often faster than answers can form. The mind tries to protect itself by preparing for every possible scenario. You may feel your thoughts racing ahead into the unknown, picturing outcomes before you even know what the next step will be. This is not a failure of faith. It is simply the mind trying to understand what the heart cannot yet hold.

What matters is not whether fear comes, but where it leads you. It can lead inward, toward isolation and self-reliance, or it can lead outward, toward God. Faith begins not when fear ends, but when you turn toward God even while afraid. Even a faint prayer, spoken through tears or whispered in the night, becomes a profound act of trust. "Lord, help me." "Stay with me." "Hold my heart." These small prayers, born from trembling rather than certainty, rise like incense to Heaven.

Look again at Jesus in Gethsemane. He does not pretend to be unafraid. He does not act invincible. He does not silence His anguish.

He falls to the ground, face to the earth, and prays with honesty. He tells the Father exactly what He feels: "Let this cup pass from Me." That prayer is not weakness. It is truth. It is love. It is relationship. Christ brings His fear to the One who loves Him. And then, in the same breath, He entrusts Himself completely: "Not My will, but Yours be done." Fear and trust are woven together in a single prayer.

This is what it looks like for the believer to pray in the valley of suffering. You can say to God, "I am scared" without shame. You can say, "I did not want this" without guilt. You can say, "Help me endure" without pretending to be strong. You can say, "I don't know how to do this" and know that God does not recoil from your weakness. Your fear becomes holy when you refuse to hide it. It becomes prayer when you hand it to Him.

Fear also reveals love. You fear because life matters. You fear because people matter. You fear because your presence in the world is bound to the hearts of those who love you. This fear is not selfish; it is relational. It comes from the deepest parts of your humanity. You want to stay. You want to live. You want to continue walking beside those who hold your heart. God sees that longing. He honours it. He understands it. Christ Himself cried out for His life in the garden, not because He lacked trust, but because He loved deeply.

Some people respond to your diagnosis by telling you to "stay strong" or "keep positive." They mean well, but these words can sometimes add weight you do not need. The Gospel does not ask you to pretend. Real strength is not the refusal to cry; it is the decision to keep walking while your tears fall. Real courage is not the absence of trembling; it is the refusal to let trembling have the final word. Heaven's saints did not walk through suffering untouched by fear. They walked through it with their eyes fixed on God.

Your fear does not surprise Him. He knew it would come. He knew the day would arrive when the news would shake you. He knew the questions that would erupt inside your heart. And He stands beside you not with disappointment but with compassion. Christ's first instinct is not to judge your fear but to enter it. He does not stand outside your pain waiting for you to improve. He steps inside it, sharing the weight, breathing peace into places fear cannot reach.

Think of the disciples on the stormy sea. They were seasoned fishermen, yet the storm terrified them. They woke Jesus not with calm faith but with panic: "Lord, do You not care that we are perishing?" Their hands shook. Their hearts raced. Their fear was not noble. Yet Christ did not condemn them. He stood and calmed the sea. He rebuked the wind, not the disciples. He spoke peace first to the storm, then to their hearts. Their trembling did not drive Him away. It drew Him near.

Your fear can draw Him near as well. It can become the place where you first sense His presence, not in dramatic visions or overwhelming feelings, but in quiet endurance, in the small ability to get through one more hour, in the courage to show up to appointments, in the strength to tell the truth about how you feel, in the grace to let others love you. These small evidences of strength are not self-manufactured; they are gifts from the God who walks with you.

Fear often intensifies at night. Darkness makes thoughts louder. The body lies still while the mind imagines possibilities. You may find it hard to rest, hard to slow your heartbeat, hard to silence what your imagination insists on repeating. God is not distant in those hours. Christ knows what it is to face the night with sorrow. He knows what it is to look ahead to suffering and feel the weight of it. He knows what it is to seek the Father with no witnesses but the stars. You do not lie awake alone. Your prayers, even if wordless, are gathered into His own.

In time, fear begins to change. It may not disappear quickly — suffering rarely works that way — but it softens under God's touch. It becomes less like a storm and more like a wave that comes and goes. You begin to notice that fear no longer controls you the way it once did. You find yourself able to sit quietly without spiralling. You discover strength for conversations you dreaded. You notice small moments of peace rising unexpectedly, like gentle interruptions of grace.

These moments do not mean the battle is over. They simply mean God is working. Often the deepest transformations happen unnoticed. The roots of trust grow in hidden soil. You might think nothing is changing, yet God is shaping your heart to endure with Him. He is giving you the grace to walk step by step, without needing to know the entire path ahead.

Fear, then, becomes a teacher. It teaches you how dependent you are on God. It teaches you how precious your life and relationships truly are. It teaches you that strength does not come from within, but from the One who holds you. It teaches you that prayer is not a performance but an act of surrender. It teaches you that the presence of God is not measured by how calm you feel, but by His unbreakable promise to remain with you.

You do not have to conquer fear to be faithful. You only have to turn toward God with the little strength you have. Even a sigh becomes a prayer. Even a tear becomes an offering. Even silence becomes communion when your heart leans toward Him in trust.

He does not despise your trembling. He receives it. He stands beside you. He carries what you cannot.

He carries what you cannot. That truth becomes clearer the longer you walk this path. At first the fear feels overwhelming, like something that has taken hold of your entire life. You may wake with it, carry it through the day, and sleep restlessly beneath its weight. Yet slowly, quietly, almost imperceptibly, you may discover something new: a strength that is not yours alone. You begin to notice that you are still standing. You are still showing up. You are still breathing and hoping, even when hope feels fragile. You are still moving forward, even when you are not sure how. This strength is grace. It is Christ within you. It is His hand beneath your trembling heart.

There is a psalm that says, "When my heart is overwhelmed, lead me to the rock that is higher than I." This is the prayer of the suffering believer. You do not ask God to remove every fear instantly. You ask Him to lift you above what you cannot bear alone. Fear makes us aware of how small we are, and yet it also reveals how near God is. You find yourself being carried when you expected to collapse. You find yourself held when you thought you would fall apart. You find that fear, instead of destroying your faith, becomes the very place where faith deepens.

Sometimes you may wonder whether God is disappointed in you for feeling afraid. You might imagine Him wanting you to be stronger, calmer, more confident. Yet the God revealed in Jesus Christ is tender with the fearful. Christ never turns away someone who approaches Him in weakness. He never demands courage before giving mercy. When Jairus, the father whose daughter was dying, came trembling to Him, Jesus did not say, "Come back when you are brave." He said, "Do not fear; only believe." Not a command to feel differently, but an invitation to lean on Him.

Those words echo through every hospital corridor, every waiting room, every sleepless night: "Do not fear; only believe." They do not erase the difficulty of what lies ahead. They simply place the weight onto stronger shoulders. Faith does not mean pretending the road will be easy. It means trusting that Christ will walk it with you.

Fear often tries to predict the future. It imagines every worst-case scenario. It leaps ahead days, weeks, months. It searches for control where no control can be found. When that happens, one of the most powerful acts of faith is to draw the mind gently back to the present moment — the only place where God's grace is actually given. Christ does not hand out tomorrow's strength today. He gives the grace needed for this hour, this breath, this step. When you stay in the present with Him, fear loses some of its power. The future, which once loomed like a shadow, becomes a place God will meet you when the time comes.

There is a quiet truth that begins to reveal itself slowly: you do not have to feel unafraid in order to be faithful. You only need to stay close. Sometimes staying close looks like prayer. Sometimes it looks like letting others pray for you when you cannot. Sometimes it looks like going to treatment even when your heart races. Sometimes it looks like getting out of bed when you would rather stay beneath the covers. Sometimes it looks like resting when you need rest. Sometimes it looks like crying. Every one of these small choices becomes an act of trust.

What God desires most is not your composure, but your surrender. He wants you to let Him hold the fear with you. He wants you to lean on Him the way a child leans on a parent after a nightmare — not because the nightmare is gone, but because someone stronger is now near. When you speak even a single word of prayer in the midst of fear, you are already living faith more deeply than you know.

In time, this trust begins to shape you. Fear may still return — sometimes sharply, sometimes quietly — but it no longer defines you. It becomes something you pass through, not something that masters you. You begin to realize that fear has not driven God away. It has drawn Him closer. He is not on the other side of your anxiety waiting for you to calm down. He sits beside you in it. He breathes peace into the spaces where your own strength ends.

The saints describe this mystery beautifully. They speak of discovering God most intimately not in moments of triumph but in moments of weakness. They describe faith not as a fortress but as an embrace. They found God not beyond fear, but within it — not because fear disappeared, but because God's presence became deeper than the fear itself. Their witness is not meant to shame you but to encourage you. What they experienced is not reserved for spiritual giants. It is offered to every believer who suffers, including you.

Fear also awakens compassion. You may find yourself seeing the suffering of others differently now. You understand their tremors, their questions, their sleepless nights, their longing for reassurance. Your heart may grow gentler. Your words may grow kinder. You may begin to notice how many people carry hidden fears of their own. In this way, the fear you experience becomes a strange foundation for mercy — the kind of mercy that sees others through God's eyes.

And while fear can make you feel isolated, it can also reveal the love around you. People who care for you may step forward in unexpected ways. Their presence may become a comfort you did not anticipate. Their small acts of kindness may lighten your days. Their prayers may carry you when your own voice is faint. Fear narrows the world, but love widens it again.

At the heart of all this stands Christ. Not far away. Not waiting at the finish line. Beside you. Within you. Carrying you. His presence does not guarantee that you will never tremble. It guarantees that you will never tremble alone. He enters your fear so that it becomes a place of encounter rather than despair. He transforms fear not by removing it, but by filling it with Himself.

This is why fear cannot be your enemy. It is not a verdict against you. It is not a sign of spiritual failure. It is part of the journey through which God will draw you closer to His heart. Fear may shake you, but it cannot separate you from Him. Nothing can. Not illness. Not uncertainty. Not weakness. Not even death. The covenant God has made with you is stronger than every fear you face.

As you move through this chapter and into the next, carry this truth gently with you: fear is allowed. Fear is expected. Fear is human. But fear does not define you. What defines you is the God who holds you. What sustains you is the grace that rises quietly within you. What strengthens you is the hand of Christ, steady even when yours trembles.

And when fear returns — as it will — remember that the first step of faith is simple: lift your eyes, even for a moment, toward the One who walks with you. You do not need to feel brave. You need only to let Him be near. Every breath taken with that intention becomes a victory of grace.

You may not be able to silence the fear, but you can place it in the hands of the One who conquered the darkness. You can whisper the simplest prayer — "Jesus, stay with me" — and know that He does. Every moment. Every night. Every step.

You will face this journey, but you will not face it alone. Fear may visit your heart, but Christ remains in it. His presence is stronger. His love is deeper. His peace, though sometimes hidden, is real. And as long as He is with you, fear can shake you, but it cannot break you.

This is the truth that will carry you forward: You are afraid, yes. But you are held.

Two

The God Who Weeps With Us

There is a moment in the Gospel when Jesus stands before a tomb, and everything in the scene feels painfully familiar to anyone who has suffered. There is sorrow. There is confusion. There are people who do not understand why God allowed this to happen. There are cries, questions, and the quiet helplessness that follows death. And right there, at the centre of the story, stands Jesus — not distant, not unshaken, not emotionally detached, but deeply moved, His eyes filling with tears. The Gospel of John tells the story with disarming simplicity: "Jesus wept" (John 11:35). These may be the shortest words in Scripture, yet they open the deepest window into the heart of God.

To understand what this means for you — for anyone walking through cancer — imagine the scene. Lazarus, the friend Jesus loved, has died. His sisters, Mary and Martha, are devastated. Martha runs to Jesus first, her voice trembling with a mixture of faith and sorrow: "Lord, if You had been here, my brother would not have died" (John 11:21). That sentence carries the weight of so many prayers spoken through tears. It is not an accusation. It is the language of grief.

It is what a heart says when it believes in God's power yet cannot understand His timing.

Mary comes later. She falls at His feet and says the same words: "Lord, if You had been here…" Her grief is so raw that she cannot finish the sentence. She sobs. The crowd around her sobs. And Jesus, seeing her tears, does something that should change forever the way we imagine God: "He was deeply moved in spirit and troubled" (John 11:33). The ancient Greek here is strong — it describes a kind of visceral, gut-level stirring. Jesus does not watch her sadness from a polite distance. He feels it. He enters it. He takes it into Himself.

Then comes the shortest verse in the Bible, the verse that reveals the very soul of God: "Jesus wept." The Son of God — the One through whom all things were made — allowed tears to fall down His face over the suffering of someone He loved. Even though He knew He would raise Lazarus moments later, He still chose to stand in the grief first. Before He brings resurrection, He shares the sorrow.

This matters for you. It matters for every person who has heard the word "cancer" and felt their world shift beneath their feet. It means that your tears are not wasted. They are not ignored. They are not signs of weak faith. They are invitations — quiet, painful invitations — that draw Christ to your side. St. Augustine once wrote, "He wept as a man, so that you might not be ashamed to weep" (*Tractates on John*). Christ dignifies human tears by shedding them Himself.

When you suffer, you may instinctively think that God is far away. Pain does that. It narrows the world and makes Heaven feel unreachable. Yet Scripture tells a different story. It shows a God who steps into human grief, who sits beside the weeping, who allows His own heart to break with theirs. The prophet Isaiah foretold this long before Christ came: He is the "Man of Sorrows, acquainted with grief" (Isaiah 53:3). Not a stranger to sorrow. Acquainted with it. Familiar with it. Close to it.

Some people imagine God as unmoved, untouched, serenely above human suffering. But that is not the God revealed in Jesus Christ. When Christ stands before Lazarus' tomb, He does not teach from a distance. He does not say, "Be strong, everything will be alright." He weeps. This means that God is not embarrassed by your tears. He is not waiting for you to become stoic or composed. He meets you exactly where you hurt.

Your own experience of cancer may feel like its own kind of tomb scene. There is grief — grief for the life you had, for the strength you once carried, for the fears your family now holds. There is confusion — Why did this happen? Why now? Why me? There may even be moments when you echo Martha and Mary: "Lord, if You had been here..." If You had intervened earlier... If You had protected me... If You had answered my prayers differently...

The Gospel does not rebuke these questions. It holds them. Christ stands in the middle of them. St. John Chrysostom, reflecting on this moment, said that Christ "mixed His tears with human tears, showing His love" (*Homily on John*). Your questions do not frighten God. Your grief does not drive Him away. Your sorrow does not make Him silent. Instead, it draws Him close.

When you imagine Christ approaching Lazarus' tomb, do not see only a story from long ago. See the God who approaches you in the same way. He does not rush to the miracle. He does not skip over the sorrow. He stands with you first, His heart aligned with yours. This is why the Church has always taught that Christ is not only our Redeemer but also our Companion. He is Emmanuel — "God with us" (Matthew 1:23) — not only in joy but especially in suffering.

Cancer may feel like a private grief that no one else can truly enter. Even those who love you deeply cannot fully understand what you carry. But Christ can. He does. He carries the knowledge of what it is to be human, to suffer, to face the shadow of death. The Letter to the Hebrews says, "We do not have a high priest who is unable to sympathise with our weaknesses" (Hebrews 4:15). Christ does not merely observe your pain; He sympathises with it. The original word means "to suffer alongside." This is who He is.

Sometimes you may feel guilty for crying or collapsing emotionally. You may think, "I should be stronger," or "I don't want to upset my family," or "I don't want to look like I'm losing hope." But Jesus did not scold Mary for falling at His feet. He did not pressure Martha into pretending to be strong. He simply received them. God does not ask you to hide your pain from Him. He asks you to bring it to Him.

One of the most comforting details of the Lazarus story is this: Jesus arrives four days after Lazarus' death. Four days is long enough for hope to have dimmed, long enough for the finality of the situation to settle in, long enough for the mourners to have begun letting reality sink in. Christ does not rush. He does not work on our timetable. But His timing is never the timing of indifference. Every step He takes toward that tomb is motivated by love.

Your own journey may feel like that — long, slow, heavy with waiting. Waiting for test results. Waiting for treatments. Waiting for recovery. Waiting for a moment of peace. But waiting does not mean God is absent. His love moves toward you even when you cannot feel it. Just as Jesus walked toward Bethany, He walks toward every place where His children suffer.

And then, in front of that tomb, He weeps. This is the God who created stars. The God who sustains galaxies. The God who commands life and death. He cries. The divine tears fall onto the dust of human sorrow. There is no other religion in the world that dares to say this — that God Himself weeps. Not in metaphor. Not in symbol. In flesh and blood.

For anyone suffering with cancer, this means that your sorrow is not a sign that God has turned His face away. It means the opposite:

God is close enough to share it.

St. Ephrem the Syrian wrote, "When He saw our affliction, He became afflicted for our sake" (*Hymns on the Nativity*). This is not poetic exaggeration. It is the literal truth of the Incarnation. Christ enters every place where humanity hurts. Not as a spectator. As one who loves.

And now, in your suffering, He weeps with you. He sits beside you. He holds what feels too heavy for you to hold alone.

He does not leave before the miracle. He stays until the end.

Christ's tears at Lazarus' tomb are not only an expression of human emotion; they are a revelation of divine compassion. They show that God does not transform suffering from a distance. He transforms it from within. Before He calls Lazarus out of the grave, before He speaks a single word of resurrection, He first stands with the grieving. He honours their pain. He allows their sorrow to become His own. This is how God moves: not as a magician performing a trick, but as a Father who joins His children in the dust before He lifts them out of it.

For anyone facing cancer, this order matters profoundly. God is not waiting on the other side of the trial, inviting you to catch up when you are "strong enough." He is not overlooking your suffering, nor expecting you to endure it in silence. He comes into the hospital room. Into the fear. Into the long nights. Into the quiet moments where your heart feels heavy. Christ enters grief before He transforms it. And because He enters it, grief becomes a place of encounter rather than abandonment.

There is a line from St. Gregory of Nazianzus that captures this mystery: "What has not been assumed has not been healed." Christ assumes not only human flesh but the full experience of human sorrow. He allows Himself to feel what we feel so that nothing in our humanity is left untouched by His healing presence. This includes your sadness. This includes your tears. This includes the moments when your heart feels too fragile to hold the weight of suffering.

When you cry over the changes in your body, Christ understands. When you grieve the life you once lived, He understands. When you fear for your family or feel the uncertainty of what lies ahead, He understands. He has walked into death itself. He has faced the silence of the tomb. He has encountered the anguish of those who loved Him. There is no valley of sorrow that He has not already entered.

One of the quiet tragedies of suffering is the sense of isolation it brings. Even surrounded by people, even loved deeply, you may feel that no one fully understands what you are going through. And in a human sense, this is true. No two experiences of illness are identical. No one else feels precisely what you feel, carries precisely what you carry, or sees the world from exactly where you stand. But Christ does. He knows your inner life completely, not in a distant, theological sense, but in a profoundly personal one.

The Letter to the Hebrews says that Christ became like us "in every respect" (Hebrews 2:17) so that He could be the perfect companion in suffering. He is not a distant deity. He is Emmanuel — God with us — in the truest sense. When He weeps, He is not performing empathy. He is revealing His heart. And that heart has room for the full weight of your sorrow.

This truth reshapes how you see your own tears. They are not failures. They are prayers. They are places where your humanity cries out for divine presence. St. Bernard of Clairvaux once wrote, "The tears of the sorrowful are the wine of angels." Meaning: Heaven does not despise grief; Heaven receives it. Even your weakest moments have value before God. Even your tears become part of your relationship with Him.

When cancer presses heavily upon you, you may be tempted to think that your sorrow burdens God. But Christ's tears show the opposite. He is not burdened by your pain; He is drawn to it. He does not recoil;

He approaches. He does not stand apart; He stands within. Your grief does not exhaust Him. It calls forth His tenderness.

Think again of the moment when Mary fell at His feet. She did not bring Him a polished prayer. She brought Him her heartbreak. She collapsed, weeping, unable to hold herself together. And Jesus responded not with frustration, but with compassion. He felt her sorrow so deeply that He wept. This means that what you feel right now — the grief, the confusion, the ache of it all — is not something you must hide from God. He invites you to bring it, just as Mary did.

Sometimes, when suffering stretches over weeks or months, grief becomes layered. There is the physical grief — the fatigue, the pain, the loss of strength. There is the emotional grief — the uncertainty, the worry, the sense of vulnerability. There is the relational grief — watching loved ones share the burden, worrying about how your illness affects them. And there is the spiritual grief — wondering where God is in all of this.

Every one of these layers matters to Him. Christ's weeping shows that none of them are ignored.

You might feel guilty for grieving. You might think, "Other people have it worse," or "I should be grateful," or "I shouldn't feel this sad." But grief is not a measuring contest. It is the love you carry mourning what has changed. St. Augustine said, "The measure of love is the measure of one's sorrow when the beloved is lost." In other words, you grieve because you care — and God honours that.

Christ does not rush your grieving. He does not say, "Hurry up and trust Me." He does not force resurrection before the heart is ready. He stands with you, patient, tender, steady. He lets you cry. He lets you speak. He lets you collapse at His feet. He lets you feel the weight of what has changed. And then — slowly — He brings light into the darkness.

This is how grace works: not by erasing the sorrow, but by

transforming it from within.

When Jesus wept at Lazarus' tomb, the people around Him said, "See how He loved him!" (John 11:36). This is what your life, even now, reveals to Heaven. Christ's compassion toward you is not theoretical. It is visible. If the saints could see Christ's heart toward you right now, they would say the same words: "See how He loves them!" Not because suffering is good — it isn't. Not because cancer is meaningful — it isn't. But because Christ's love shines even more brightly when your life passes through the shadows.

Your grief, then, becomes a place of revelation. Not a revelation of your weakness, but of His nearness. Not a revelation of God's silence, but of His tenderness. Not a revelation of abandonment, but of companionship.

If you listen closely in the silence of your hardest moments, you may sense something unexpected: Christ's presence, not loud or dramatic, but steady. A presence that does not remove all pain but makes the carrying of it possible. A presence that whispers, "I am here. I am with you. I am not leaving." This is not imagination. This is the truth of the Gospel lived out in your life.

What Christ did for Mary and Martha, He does for you. He stands beside your sorrow. He lets His heart be moved by your grief. He weeps with you. And He accompanies you until the moment when He will speak restoration — whether in this life or in the next.

You may not yet feel the resurrection. You may not yet see the miracle. You may still be standing in the place of tears. But Christ is standing there too, and that changes everything. St. Ephrem said that when Jesus stood at the tomb of Lazarus, "He made the tomb a bridal chamber," meaning He turned a place of death into a place of hope. He can do the same with your suffering. He can transform what feels like pure loss into a place where grace enters, where love deepens, where God reveals Himself in ways He never could have otherwise.

This does not mean your suffering is good. It means Christ is good. It means His presence fills even the worst places with a love that does not break, does not fade, does not abandon.

Cancer does not make God indifferent. It makes Him draw nearer.

And so, when the grief comes — as it will — remember Lazarus' tomb. Remember the tears of God. Remember that Christ's heart is never far from yours, especially in sorrow. Remember that the One who will one day speak life into every grave is the same One who weeps with you now. His compassion is not temporary. His love is not fragile. His presence is not conditional.

You may feel crushed, but you are not alone. You may feel sorrowful, but you are not unseen. You may feel overwhelmed, but you are held by the God who enters grief before He transforms it.

And one day, just as surely as He called Lazarus out of the tomb, He will call every tear out of your story. Until that day comes, He stands beside you, in every breath, with a heart that knows sorrow and a love that will see you through it.

Three

When We Ask "Why Me?"

There comes a point in every season of suffering when the heart cannot help but ask the question it has been carrying in silence: "Why me?" It does not come from anger at first, nor from rebellion, nor from any rejection of God. It comes from a place so deep that words barely reach it — a place where fear, grief, confusion, and longing all mix together. A place where life suddenly feels unfamiliar and fragile. A place where you cannot help but ask how something like this has happened to you. The question rises naturally the way breath rises in the chest: without permission, without pretence, without needing to be polished. It is a human question, spoken by the heart before the mind knows what to do with it.

If you have asked it — quietly in the night, aloud through tears, or even in the privacy of your thoughts — you should know this first: you are not alone. The Bible is full of this question. The saints are full of this question. And God, far from being offended by it, receives it. "Why me?" is not the language of unbelief. It is the language of relationship. It is the cry of someone who expects God to care.

One of the most striking examples of this cry appears in the life of Job. Job suffers in ways that feel overwhelming — physically, emotionally, relationally, spiritually. He loses nearly everything: family, livelihood, health, peace. And his first words after the shock is not a polished theological reflection. It is grief. It is lament. It is a heart struggling to hold what has collapsed around it. Job cries out, "Why did I not die at birth?" (Job 3:11). A few verses later he adds, "What is man, that You make so much of him… and that You test him every moment?" (Job 7:17–18). These are not polite prayers. These are raw, agonizing questions from someone who believes God is real and wonders why God has allowed so much pain.

Yet the remarkable thing about Job's story is that God does not rebuke him for asking these questions. When God finally speaks at the end of the book, He says that Job "has spoken rightly" (Job 42:7). How can this be? Because Job does not turn away from God with his pain — he brings his pain to God. Job's "Why me?" was not disbelief; it was dialogue. It was a heart refusing to let silence sever the relationship.

The same pattern appears in the Psalms, the prayerbook of the Bible. If you open the Psalms expecting serene prayers filled with perfect trust, you will be surprised. Nearly a third of the Psalms begin in anguish. "Why, O Lord, do You stand far off?" (Psalm 10:1). "How long, O Lord? Will You forget me forever?" (Psalm 13:1). "Why have You forgotten me? Why must I walk about mournfully?" (Psalm 42:9). The most shocking of all, the Psalm Jesus Himself prayed from the Cross: "My God, My God, why have You forsaken me?" (Psalm 22:1). These are not whispers of people trying to hide their sorrow from God. These are cries of people who believe so deeply in God's love that they dare to bring even their confusion to Him.

St. Augustine once wrote, "You hear the cry of the heart, O Lord, whether it is spoken aloud or kept in silence" (*Confessions*). This is the reassurance Scripture gives: God is not surprised by your "Why me?"

He is not threatened by it. He is not angered by it. He hears it as the cry of someone who still turns in His direction.

Perhaps the most striking example of this silent cry is Mary standing beneath the Cross. Scripture shows her there, remaining close to Jesus as He suffers. She does not speak a word, yet her very presence is a question: Why must my Son endure this? Why must I witness it? Why has this road been given to us? Simeon had foretold years earlier, "A sword will pierce your own soul also" (Luke 2:35). Now the sword has come, and Mary is living the mystery of suffering without explanation. She is the model believer — the one whose "yes" to God was perfect — yet even she passes through a valley she could not understand. Her silence beneath the Cross is the silence of all who suffer and cannot find words.

This should comfort you, not frighten you. The holiest woman in history endured the darkest silence without losing her faith. The holiest man in history cried out the harshest lament from a Cross. Scripture is not ashamed of these moments. Neither should you be.

When cancer enters a life, the question "Why me?" rises naturally. You might ask it while sitting at home after receiving the diagnosis, replaying the doctor's words in your mind. You might ask it while looking in the mirror and seeing the changes in your body. You might ask it when you watch your family worry, or when you face treatment, or when your strength is low, or when you wake at night with the weight of uncertainty pressing upon your chest. The question does not come because you have lost your faith. It comes because suffering has touched something sacred — your hope, your identity, your sense of security, your longing for life, your love for those around you.

There is something important to understand here: "Why me?" is not a challenge thrown at God. It is not rebellion. It is not spiritual immaturity. It is the instinct of the heart to seek meaning in the midst of pain. It is the soul reaching upward for the God it believes is there, asking for light in a place that has become dark. It is the prayer of someone who refuses to hide from God.

If you did not believe God loved you, you would not ask Him these things. If you did not believe He had power, His silence would not trouble you. If you did not believe He was good, your suffering would not feel like such a mystery. "Why me?" is the prayer of someone who expects God to care. It is the language of a relationship that is alive, even when wounded. As Pope John Paul II wrote, "In suffering, the individual opens himself to the working of God's saving powers" (*Salvifici Doloris*, 23). That opening often begins with this very question.

Some Christians feel guilty for asking God "Why me?" They imagine that real faith never questions, never trembles, never wonders. But the Bible gives a different lesson. The people who questioned God the most — Job, David, Jeremiah — were often the ones God praised the most. Their questions were not insults; they were invitations. They kept the relationship alive. St. Gregory the Great said something beautiful: "Tears are the soul's testimony that it seeks God." Even your confusion becomes a kind of longing for the One who can make sense of what feels senseless.

It is important to say this clearly: your suffering is not a punishment. God is not targeting you. God is not balancing some cosmic scale. Cancer is not a sign that God is disappointed in you or that you have failed Him. Illness enters the world through frailty, genetics, brokenness, and mystery — but never as evidence that God has withdrawn His love. Jesus Himself refuted this idea when His disciples asked whether the man born blind was suffering because of sin. Christ answered plainly, "Neither this man nor his parents sinned" (John 9:3). Suffering is not proof of guilt. It is part of the mystery God enters in order to redeem.

And this leads to another truth: God hears your "Why me?" even when He does not answer it immediately. This can be frustrating. We want clarity. We want explanations. We want God to draw back the curtain of mystery and tell us exactly what He is doing. But in Scripture, God rarely answers the question "why" in the moment suffering occurs. Instead, He answers with His presence.

When Job pours out all his questions, God finally speaks — but not with an explanation. He reveals Himself. Job is given not an answer, but a Person. And that Person is enough to steady him. Job says, "I had heard of You by the hearing of the ear, but now my eye sees You" (Job 42:5). What changed him was not information but encounter.

You may feel that God is silent right now. You may feel you have asked your question into an empty sky. But silence does not mean absence. In the Bible, silence often precedes revelation. Elijah heard God not in the wind, nor in the fire, nor in the earthquake, but in "a still small voice" (1 Kings 19:12). Abraham walked three days in silence toward Moriah before God revealed the ram. The disciples sat in the silence of Holy Saturday before Easter dawned. Silence is not the end of the story. It is often the threshold of something sacred.

And so your "Why me?" is not a prayer God ignores. It is a prayer He holds — gently, patiently, lovingly — until the moment your heart is ready for what comes next.

God receives your question long before you ever hear His answer. Sometimes He answers slowly, quietly, through moments of grace that appear unexpectedly. Sometimes He answers through the compassion of those around you — a friend who calls at the right hour, a family member who holds your hand, a nurse who treats you with dignity, a doctor whose wisdom steadies your fear. Sometimes He answers through Scripture, where ancient words suddenly feel written for you. And sometimes He answers not with clarity but with strength — the strength to live through a day you feared you could not endure. These small mercies are not accidental. They are God's silent replies, ways of saying, "I am here. I have not forgotten you."

But even when these moments come, the heart may still return to the question: "Why me?" This is part of being human. The question is not something you ask once and resolve forever. It returns as new challenges appear. It rises on difficult days. It emerges when pain deepens or when hope feels thin. It surfaces when you see your loved ones suffering with you, and you wonder why this burden must fall on the people you care about most. It is not a failure to ask again. It is simply the heart speaking honestly in the moment it finds itself.

If we look again at Scripture, we realise that God does not merely tolerate this honesty — He invites it. He placed the Psalms of lament in the centre of the Bible so that every generation could learn how to bring sorrow to Him. He preserved the cries of Job so suffering people would know they are not alone. He allowed the anguished prayers of the prophets to remain, because suffering is not a defect in faith — it is the place where faith speaks most truthfully. C.S. Lewis once said that prayer is not about telling God what He does not know, but about "unlearning our disguises." "Why me?" unpacks the disguise. It reveals the heart.

But the heart must hear another truth as well: the presence of suffering does not erase the presence of God's love. Disease is not the final word. Pain is not a verdict. If you belong to God — and you do — then nothing that happens in your life is outside the reach of His compassion. St. Paul reminds us that nothing "in all creation will be able to separate us from the love of God" (Romans 8:39). Not suffering. Not fear. Not illness. Not uncertainty. Not even the question "Why me?" can separate you from Him. If anything, that question is the stretch of your soul toward His.

There is a moment in the Gospels when Jesus meets a man who has been sick for thirty-eight years (John 5). Jesus does not begin with a lecture or an explanation. He begins with a question: "Do you want to be healed?" The man does not respond with a perfect expression of trust. He complains. He explains how everyone else reaches the water before him. He voices his frustration, his helplessness, his sadness. And Jesus does not rebuke him. Instead, He heals him. This is the pattern: honesty leads to encounter; encounter leads to grace.

Your honesty — your "Why me?" — is not a barrier to God. It is a door. Behind it stands a God who understands your sorrow more deeply than you do, a God who has walked the path of suffering Himself, a God who knows the weight of unanswered questions. Christ on the Cross experienced the deepest form of human anguish, and in that moment He prayed the Psalm of lament: "My God, My God, why have You forsaken Me?" (Psalm 22:1; Matthew 27:46). He did not recite a triumphal prayer. He did not quote a theology textbook. He cried out the very question that emerges from the heart of every suffering human being.

Why did He pray those words? Not because He doubted the Father's love — He knew the Father's plan more than anyone. He prayed them so that no one who prays them in their suffering ever prays alone. When you ask, "Why me?" Christ stands beside you, saying, "I have spoken this question too. I have made it holy." The Cross is the place where your question meets His, where your sorrow touches His, where your fear is embraced by a love stronger than death.

But here is the quiet truth: though God hears the question, He does not always answer it in the way we expect. Job never hears why he suffered — he only meets God. Mary never hears a verbal explanation beneath the Cross — she only receives her Son into her arms. The psalmists often cry into silence, but their cries end in trust, not because they understand, but because they sense God drawing near.

The pattern in Scripture is clear: God may not answer "Why me?" directly, but He answers with Himself. He gives His presence before He gives His explanation. He strengthens the heart before He clarifies the mystery. He transforms suffering before He tells you its purpose

— and sometimes the purpose is only understood in eternity.

This means you are free to ask the question without waiting for a perfect response. You can speak honestly without fear of offending God. Your relationship with Him is not fragile. It can withstand sorrow. It can withstand confusion. It can withstand nights when you do not know what to pray. God is not surprised by your humanity. He created you with a heart that asks, that longs, that aches, that seeks.

If you could see the full tapestry of your life — every thread of grace woven through suffering, every act of love that will emerge from this season, every moment of compassion your illness will awaken in others, every hidden strengthening God is accomplishing in your soul — you would see that your story is held by hands far gentler than you imagined. But for now, you see only a fragment. And so the heart asks, "Why me?" This is not a failure. It is faith reaching in the dark.

Some people fear that asking this question is a sign of weak belief. But the opposite is true. Only someone who believes in God's goodness feels wounded when suffering appears. Only someone who trusts God feels confused when life derails. The very fact that you bring your question to God shows that your relationship with Him is alive. Silence would reveal indifference. The question reveals love.

And yet the heart needs reassurance: God is not punishing you. God is not disappointed in you. God has not withdrawn from you. God is not testing you to see how much you can take. Cancer is not a divine calculation. It is a human tragedy — and God meets human tragedy with compassion, not condemnation.

Christ Himself confirms this in the simplest way: He never turned away a suffering person. Not once. Not in the Gospels. Not in all of Scripture. He did not ask them to explain their illness. He did not measure their spiritual performance. He did not evaluate their worthiness. He looked at them with love, listened to their cries, and stood with them in their pain. He healed many, comforted all, and condemned none. The God who behaved this way on earth behaves no differently now.

So when you ask "Why me?" picture Christ beside you, not distant. Picture Him listening, not judging. Picture Him entering your sorrow, not stepping back from it. Picture Him holding the question with you, not silencing it. Picture Him saying, "I hear you. I am here. I am with you in this."

This chapter is not meant to answer the question in a way that removes all mystery. Instead, it is meant to tell you that the question is welcomed, the tears are seen, the confusion is understood, and the God who loves you is not offended by your pain. He is moved by it. He receives it. He walks within it.

In time — perhaps sooner, perhaps later, perhaps only in eternity — He will reveal what this suffering has opened in your life. But until that day, He accompanies you with a compassion more tender than any explanation, with a presence more healing than any argument, with a love deeper than any answer you hoped for.

And this is why you can ask your question without fear:

Your "Why me?" begins a conversation, not a separation.

It draws you closer, not further.

It invites God into the place where your heart hurts most.

He does not turn away.

He does not ask you to hide your sorrow.

He does not demand heroic serenity.

He simply stays.

And sometimes, that is the first, most important answer of all.

Four

Suffering Does Not Mean God Has Left

There are few wounds more painful than the sense that God has gone quiet. When suffering enters a life — especially the kind of suffering that comes with cancer — the heart often finds itself asking not only *why* this has happened but *where God has gone*. It is a question that rises not with anger, but with ache. You pray, yet nothing seems to move. You cry, yet Heaven feels still. You reach for God, yet your hands close on silence. And there comes a point when the whisper grows louder inside: *Has God left me? Am I walking this road alone?*

It is a terrible lie because it attaches itself to our deepest fear: the fear of abandonment. Human hearts are wired for connection; we are made for presence. Children turn instinctively to their parents when frightened not because they expect an explanation, but because they expect a nearness that reassures. Suffering, however, often interrupts that instinct. It clouds our vision. It disturbs our peace. It plays tricks with our perception of God. The one thing we long to feel — His closeness — is the one thing we struggle to sense.

Yet the first truth this chapter must speak is this: the feeling of abandonment is not the fact of abandonment.

In Scripture, the people God loves most often feel abandoned precisely at the moment God is closest. The psalmist cries out, "Why do You hide Your face from me?" (Psalm 88:14). That line could have been written yesterday by anyone battling illness. Yet the same psalmist, in another moment of clarity, says, "I said in my alarm, 'I am cut off from Your sight,' but You heard my cry for mercy" (Psalm 31:22). Notice that: *I felt abandoned... but You heard me.* Scripture does not hide the tension between what the heart feels and what God is doing.

And perhaps that is where we must begin — with the understanding that our spiritual senses are often the least reliable during suffering. Pain narrows the world. It exhausts the emotions. It alters the mind. It can make prayer feel impossible and God feel silent. But silence, as the Bible reveals again and again, is not the same thing as absence. Silence is often the doorway through which God prepares a deeper work.

Think of Job. So much of Job's suffering unfolds in silence. God does not appear immediately. He does not explain Himself. He does not rescue Job from the moment the pain begins. Yet Job is not abandoned. When God finally speaks, He says something astonishing: Job "has spoken rightly" (Job 42:7). How could Job's anguished cries be *right*? Because they were spoken into the relationship. Even when Job thought God had turned away, he kept addressing God. The silence was not abandonment; it was a mystery of timing. God was nearer than Job felt, shaping him, enlarging him, preparing him.

Or consider Joseph. Betrayed by his brothers, thrown into a pit, sold into slavery, and then unjustly imprisoned. If ever there were a life that seemed abandoned by God, it was Joseph's. Yet Scripture says something quietly stunning: "The Lord was with Joseph" (Genesis 39:21). Not after the suffering. Not once the miracle arrived. In the pit. In the cell. In the place where nothing felt holy or hopeful or redeemable. The presence of God accompanied Joseph even when

Joseph had no earthly reason to feel it.

And then Israel in Egypt — centuries of silence. Centuries where the cries of the children of Abraham seemed to disappear into the sky. Yet when God speaks to Moses, His first words reveal the truth: "I have surely seen the affliction of My people... I have heard their cry... I know their sufferings" (Exodus 3:7). What felt like abandonment was, in reality, unseen accompaniment. God had never removed His gaze.

These stories matter because they reveal something essential for anyone walking the road of cancer: God's silence is not God's departure. The God who was with Joseph in a prison is the God who is with you in the hospital room. The God who listened to Israel's cries through centuries of slavery is the God who listens to you tonight. The God who remained close to Job even when Job felt forsaken is the same God who remains close to you even now, even if every spiritual sense in you feels numb.

Scripture builds this pattern slowly: the moments when God seems most hidden are often the moments when He is doing His most important work. Elijah discovers God not in the wind, nor the earthquake, nor the fire, but "in a still small voice" (1 Kings 19:12). Sometimes the presence of God becomes so quiet that only faith, not feeling, can detect it.

But the heart of this chapter is not found in Joseph, or in Elijah, or even in Job. It is found on a hill outside Jerusalem, in the last hours of Jesus' earthly life. It is found in the cry that tears through the Gospels like a wound in the sky: "My God, My God, why have You forsaken Me?" (Matthew 27:46).

These are not merely the words of a dying man. They are the words of God made flesh entering the full depth of human suffering — entering not only physical agony but the spiritual desolation that often accompanies it. Jesus is quoting the opening line of Psalm 22, the psalm of abandonment. By praying it, He takes upon Himself the very question that emerges from your heart: *Where is God? Has He left me? Does He still hear me?*

The early Fathers of the Church wrestled with this moment. St. Athanasius said Christ speaks these words "in the voice of humanity," meaning He takes our deepest wound — the fear of divine abandonment — and makes it His own. St. Augustine said Christ prays in "our weak human nature," entering even the emotional darkness we cannot escape. Christ does not cry out because the Father has abandoned Him. Christ cries out because He has descended into the place where you feel abandoned, so that no one who enters that place will find it empty.

This is the miracle hidden inside suffering:

Christ has stood where you stand.

He has prayed what you pray.

He has felt what you feel.

He has entered the darkness so that the darkness is no longer a place of isolation but a place where He waits for you.

When you feel that God has stepped back from your life, when prayer feels dry, when loneliness expands inside you, when you ask why Heaven is so quiet, you are not stepping outside the life of faith. You are stepping into the very place Christ sanctified on the Cross. John Paul II put it this way: "No one suffers alone. Christ suffers with them." Those are not poetic words; they are theological truth. The Redeemer does not rescue from a distance — He climbs down into the pit.

And there, in the silence where we expect to find emptiness, we find Him.

But here is the difficulty: when cancer brings exhaustion, anxiety, pain, appointments, scans, long nights, and days where strength feels thin, your heart may still whisper: *But why can't I feel God? Why doesn't He comfort me like before? Why has prayer become so hard?* These questions cut deeply because they touch the spiritual core of the person.

It is one thing to suffer physically. It is another to suffer spiritually, to feel as though the One you love has grown distant.

Yet spiritual dryness is not abandonment. It is a known path in the Bible. The saints walked it. The prophets walked it. Even Jesus walked it. The absence of spiritual consolation is not the absence of God. Often it is a sign that God is drawing you more deeply into trust — not the trust that relies on feelings, but the trust that relies on His covenant promise.

And here is the promise:

"I will never leave you nor forsake you." (Hebrews 13:5)

Not "I will stay as long as you feel Me."

Not "I will stay as long as you remain strong."

Not "I will stay as long as you pray beautifully."

Just this:

I will never leave you.

The God who speaks those words does not break His promises. Not in Scripture. Not in history. Not in your life.

But suffering creates fog, and in the fog, promises can be hard to see. You may feel as though you're walking through thick darkness, unable to sense God's presence. Yet God is not measured by feeling. Feeling is fickle. Presence is not. The baby in a mother's arms may be too young to recognise the embrace — but the embrace remains. Sometimes we are the baby. We cannot perceive what holds us. But we are held nonetheless.

Your suffering may not offer spiritual sweetness right now. You may feel dry, empty, numb. But dryness does not repel God. It draws Him. He is close to the broken-hearted (Psalm 34:18), not just the joyful-hearted. The emptiness you feel does not scare Him; it invites Him. He meets you where your strength ends. He fills what you cannot. He remains when you feel nothing.

And this is where the chapter must enter your story more directly:

cancer often amplifies the sense of abandonment. You may go through long stretches where prayer feels flat, Scripture feels distant, and spiritual consolation feels out of reach. You may wonder why God, who once felt so close, now feels invisible. You may feel that your prayers bounce back unheard. You may sit in waiting rooms or lie awake at night thinking, *Lord, where are You?*

Those moments hurt. They cut deeply. They feel like betrayal. But they are not betrayal. They are the Cross — the place where Christ proves that the silence of God is still the place of God.

What feels like abandonment is often union.

What feels like emptiness is often purification.

What feels like distance is often closeness too deep for the senses to detect.

You cannot see roots growing under the soil, yet the tree depends on them.

You cannot hear your heart beating at night, yet it sustains you.

You cannot feel God in every moment, yet He is nearer to you now than you have ever been to yourself.

You do not have to sense Him to be held by Him.

You do not have to hear Him to be guided by Him.

You do not have to feel Him to belong to Him.

And you do.

There is a moment in every believer's life when faith must learn to stand not on emotion, but on the sheer truthfulness of God. That moment often arrives in suffering. It is not a punishment. It is not proof of spiritual failure. It is the maturation of a relationship. When God allows silence, He is not turning away; He is deepening your capacity to trust that love remains even when it is not felt.

Cancer accelerates this experience in ways nothing else does. There are days when your strength feels thin, when you cannot pray with the clarity or confidence you once had, when fear rises without permission, when your heart feels tired from holding so much uncertainty. On those days, your thoughts may whisper, *If God were with me, wouldn't I feel Him? Wouldn't I sense something? Wouldn't He make this easier?*

But this is where the wisdom of Scripture comes to comfort you. The Bible reveals that God's greatest works often unfold in silence. When the seed is planted in the earth, it disappears from view. It lies in darkness, unseen, covered by soil. No one would guess that within that darkness life is forming, roots are strengthening, and the future is being prepared. Jesus uses this very image: "Unless a grain of wheat falls into the earth and dies, it remains alone; but if it dies, it bears much fruit" (John 12:24). The darkness around the seed is not abandonment; it is preparation. The same is true of the darkness that sometimes surrounds your soul.

God is doing His work in the hidden places. His silence is not neglect. It is a holy mystery — one that every saint has walked through. St. Thérèse of Lisieux, whose faith was luminous, wrote near the end of her life that it felt as though "the heavens were closed" and God had stepped back. Yet she knew by faith that He was nearer than ever. St. Teresa of Calcutta passed through decades of interior dryness, yet she radiated Christ's presence more than most people on earth. The saints teach us something profound: feeling abandoned and being abandoned are not the same thing. God remains faithful even when the emotions fall silent.

Think of a parent sitting beside a child who is too ill or exhausted to notice their embrace. The child may not feel the closeness. They may not respond. But nothing has changed in the parent's heart. The love is constant, the presence unbroken. Much of our relationship with God in suffering resembles that scene. We cannot always sense the One who holds us, but the holding does not stop.

Even Christ entered this silent mystery. When He cried, "My God, My God, why have You forsaken Me?" He was not abandoned by the

Father. He was stepping into the full depth of the human experience — taking on not only our sins, but our sense of separation, our fear of God's absence, our cry in the night. He takes the "feeling" of abandonment so that He can fill that space with Himself. It means that when you feel alone, you are standing on holy ground — the ground Christ has entered. You are not isolated. You are accompanied by the One who knows this terrain better than anyone.

If Christ has stepped into the feeling of abandonment, then your own experience of that feeling is not a sign that God has left you. It is a sign that Christ is uniting you to Himself in a profound way. He draws closest to us not when we feel strong, but when we feel broken. The Cross is proof. The Resurrection is the promise.

And this brings us to the truth that suffering wants to hide from you: God does His deepest work in the moments when He seems most absent. Look at the greatest miracle in all of history — the Resurrection. When did it unfold? During Holy Saturday, the day when the disciples felt utterly abandoned, when God seemed silent and still. Behind the silence, something unimaginable was taking place. Life was conquering death. Hope was being reborn. Heaven was touching earth. None of it could be seen. None of it could be felt. But all of it was real.

Your suffering has its own Holy Saturday. A time when the world feels dim, when God feels far, when your spirit feels stretched thin. But the Christian learns that silence is not inactivity; it is mystery. It is the hidden place where God does what only God can do — strengthen the heart, deepen the soul, enlarge the capacity to love, prepare the ground for grace.

Sometimes people imagine that if God were truly with them, suffering would be easier — lighter, more bearable, perhaps even joyful. But Scripture offers a different pattern. God's presence does not always remove pain; often it transforms pain from the inside. The presence of God does not always change the circumstances, but it changes what the circumstances do to the soul. A suffering endured with God is not the same as a suffering endured alone.

And this is where faith must return to covenant — the unbreakable relationship God initiates and sustains. In the Old Testament, God binds Himself to His people again and again with the same promise: "I will be with you." The promise is repeated to Abraham, to Isaac, to Jacob, to Moses, to Joshua, to David, to Israel in exile. God never promises an easy life. He promises His presence in every circumstance. When Christ arrives, He takes that ancient promise and seals it in His own blood: "Behold, I am with you always" (Matthew 28:20). Not sometimes. Not when you feel it. Always.

So if you cannot feel God today, then allow this sentence to carry you:

God is closer than your feelings.

Feelings rise and fall. Presence does not.

Feelings fluctuate. Covenant does not.

Feelings change. God does not.

There may be days when prayer feels impossible. Days when the Scriptures do not speak the way they used to. Days when your heart feels like a stone, heavy and unmoved. Days when you sit at the edge of your bed after treatment and wonder why God is not comforting you in the way you had hoped. Those are the moments when this truth becomes the anchor of your soul: God is faithful even when the senses fall silent.

Your prayer in suffering does not need to be eloquent. It can be as simple as breathing His name. It can be as unspoken as a tear. It can be as fragile as a sigh. St. Paul writes that when we do not know how to pray, "the Spirit Himself intercedes for us with sighs too deep for words" (Romans 8:26). You may think you are praying poorly, but God hears more than your words. He hears the cry of the heart.

If you cannot pray at all, Christ prays within you. If you cannot hold on to God, God holds on to you. If you feel too weak to believe, the faith of the Church surrounds you. You are carried by the prayers of the saints, by the Mass, by the love of those who lift your name before God. Heaven is busy even when you are exhausted.

And so the lie begins to lose its power: You are not abandoned.

You have not been left alone in your suffering.

God has not withdrawn His love.

If anything, suffering often reveals how deeply God has entered into your life. The God who once felt external becomes the God who now accompanies you in every breath, every treatment, every tear, every waking hour of fear. The God who once seemed to stand above your life now stands beside you in its most fragile places.

This chapter cannot promise that you will always feel God's presence — but it can promise something truer: that God's presence does not depend on your feeling. And that is good news, especially in sickness, when the emotions are too turbulent to rely on.

When you walk through the valley of the shadow of death, you walk with Someone. Even if the shadows hide Him from your eyes, they cannot hide you from His. His rod and His staff comfort you (Psalm 23:4), not because you can see them, but because He has never released you from His grasp.

You may feel alone.

You may fear being alone.

You may pray and hear nothing.

You may seek and feel nothing.

You may cry and sense nothing.

Yet Heaven whispers over your life the truth that suffering tries to drown out:

"I will never leave you nor forsake you."

Not today.

Not tomorrow.

Not in the hospital.

Not in the silence of the night.

Not in the uncertainty of the future.

Your suffering is not a sign that God has left.

It is the place where God draws nearer than you have ever known.

And if you could see — even for a moment — the One who stands beside you, the One who prays within you, the One who suffers with you, the One who shapes grace out of every hour of your pain, then the silence would no longer frighten you. You would know that silence is simply His hidden work.

You are not alone.

You have never been alone.

Not for a moment.

Not for a heartbeat.

Not for a breath.

He is here.

He remains.

And nothing — not cancer, not fear, not sorrow, not even death — can separate you from the love that holds you now and forever.

Five

When Strength Falters, Something Sacred Begins

There comes a moment in every journey through suffering when something inside begins to shift. It is not dramatic. It is not triumphant. It does not feel like revelation. It feels more like depletion — a quiet recognition that your strength is not what it once was. Part I walked through fear, grief, confusion, and the painful temptation to believe that God has stepped back. These are the honest valleys of the human heart, and Scripture never asks you to pretend they are otherwise. The God who walked with you through those valleys is the same God who now stands beside you at this threshold.

Because that is what this moment is: a threshold.

You have named your fears; you have tasted tears; you have asked questions with a trembling voice; you have wondered if silence means distance. Yet somehow, even in this, you have not walked alone. Christ met you in Gethsemane, at Lazarus' tomb, in Job's ash heap, at Mary's quiet vigil beneath the Cross. You have discovered that the Holy One does not flee from sorrow; He descends into it. You have learned that asking "Why me?" is not rebellion but relationship, the cry of a child who refuses to turn away from a Father she longs to understand. You have seen that feeling abandoned is not the same as being abandoned. God's silence is often the waiting room of grace.

All of Part I whispered a truth you may not have noticed consciously: God has already drawn near.

Yet now a different challenge begins. The emotional intensity of the diagnosis has softened into something more draining. The body weakens. Sleep becomes uncertain. Doctor's appointments multiply. Treatments take a toll. Fatigue settles in places you never expected — not only in the muscles, but in the mind, in the will, in the simple desire to face another day. Prayer, which once seemed familiar, begins to feel heavy. The heart grows quiet not because it doubts, but because it is tired.

It is precisely here — in this exhaustion — that another kind of journey begins.

Suffering changes the landscape of prayer. Before illness, prayer may have been something you could plan, something you could structure, something you could bring energy to. But when you are sick, the very energy required for prayer feels like another burden. You might lie in bed and discover that even forming the words "Lord, help me" feels like lifting a weight beyond your strength.

Yet Scripture reveals a strange and beautiful truth: the moment when your strength falters is the moment when something sacred begins.

Prayer does not wither when you are weak. Prayer becomes *truer*. The saints tell us this again and again. St. Paul wrote, "We do not know how to pray as we ought, but the Spirit Himself intercedes for us" (Romans 8:26). Prayer is not first your effort toward God; it is God's compassion moving toward you. The Spirit prays in you even when your lips cannot move. Christ prays for you even when your heart feels numb. The Father hears you even when all you can offer is your tears.

This is the mystery that Part II will unfold. Prayer in suffering is not a performance. It is not a test. It is not measured by eloquence or length. Difficulty does not diminish its power. Weakness does not diminish its worth. In fact, prayer prayed from weakness goes deeper into the heart of God than prayer prayed from comfort ever could.

There is a reason Jesus blessed the poor in spirit. The prayer of the weary, the fearful, the broken, is the prayer that rises with a purity untouched by pride. When you pray from exhaustion, you pray from the truth of your condition — and God meets the soul most tenderly in the truth.

But to understand this, you must let go of an old idea:

that prayer requires strength.

It does not.

Prayer requires honesty.

Nothing more.

If all you can manage is a whisper — *"Jesus, stay with me"* — heaven receives it as a hymn.

If all you can manage is silence — simply turning your heart toward God for a moment — that silence becomes a sanctuary.

If all you can manage is a sigh — the wordless ache of a frightened soul — Scripture tells us that even sighs are heard by the One who "collects every tear in His bottle" (Psalm 56:8).

The next part of this book will take you into this sacred territory. It will not teach you how to pray like the saints of old in their moments of triumph; it will teach you how to pray like they prayed in their moments of trial. Their greatest prayers were uttered not from mountaintops but from valleys. Elijah prayed in exhaustion beneath a broom tree. Hannah prayed in wordless anguish in the temple. David prayed in caves and deserts. Mary prayed in silence at the foot of her Son's Cross. These are the prayers God treasures — the prayers born from weakness rather than willpower.

Part II will teach you why prayer matters now more than ever, not because God needs it, but because your soul does. It will show you that silence is not God withdrawing but God drawing you deeper. It will reveal the beauty of letting others pray for you when you cannot pray for yourself. It will speak into the long nights when fear whispers too loudly and sleep refuses to come. It will teach you that prayer is not something you accomplish; prayer is something you receive.

In suffering, the heart becomes porous. It becomes open in ways it never was before. Life narrows to the essentials, and in that narrowing, something eternal slips through the cracks. You begin to see that prayer is not an obligation — it is the lifeline that keeps you tethered to God's presence when everything else feels unsteady.

Perhaps you fear you do not pray well. Perhaps you fear your faith is too small. Perhaps you fear that God expects more of you than you can give. Yet Christ never asked the sick to pray long prayers. He asked only for their trust. He asked for their presence. He asked for the small offering they could give — a reaching hand, a trembling voice, a quiet openness.

What you can offer today is enough for Him.

As you cross into Part II, you are stepping not into a school of spiritual effort but into a school of spiritual rest. A place where God does the heavy lifting. A place where the burden shifts from your shoulders to His. A place where prayer becomes a refuge, not a responsibility. A place where you discover that God is closest not when you are strong, but when you are too weak to pretend.

The valley has been real. The tears have been real. The questions have been real. The silence has been real. But now, in this next movement, you will learn something just as real — perhaps even more so:

When your strength falters, God draws nearer.

When your voice weakens, God listens more deeply.

When your heart trembles, God holds it with both hands.

Part II begins here:

with the truth that your weakness is not an obstacle to prayer —

it is the doorway into a prayer more profound than you have ever known.

When you are ready, we will walk through that doorway together.

II

WHEN THE BODY WEAKENS, THE HEART LEARNS TO PRAY

Six

When Strength Fades, Prayer Begins

There comes a moment in every season of suffering when prayer no longer feels like something we choose but something we cling to. It is not the prayer of a strong person standing upright, composed and ready. It is the prayer of someone lying on their side in a hospital bed, unsure of what tomorrow will bring, too drained to form more than a whisper. There is a tenderness in that moment, though it rarely feels tender. The body is tired. The mind feels slow. The heart is stretched thin. What once felt natural now feels distant. You may find yourself thinking, "I used to know how to pray… why is it so hard now?" That thought often carries shame, as if weakness somehow disqualifies you from speaking to God. Yet the surprising truth of Scripture, repeated across every century of faith, is that weakness does not hinder prayer; weakness makes it more true. When cancer drains strength from the body, it removes a thousand illusions from the soul. You begin to see prayer not as a discipline but as a lifeline. You begin to understand that God is not waiting for polished words or spiritual energy. He is waiting for the heart that simply turns toward Him, even if the turning is slow and small.

Before illness, many people think of prayer as something they do for God. In suffering, you discover that prayer is something God does in you. The Psalms are full of people who prayed at the end of themselves: "My strength fails," "My tears have been my food day and night," "Out of the depths I cry to You." These are not the prayers of the spiritually strong. They are the prayers of the spiritually honest. And God preserves them in Scripture because He wants you to know that He receives such prayers with a tenderness beyond all telling. Illness does not make prayer harder; illness makes prayer purer. The heart that has no energy left for performance, no space for pretending, no interest in impressing anyone—including God—is the heart that finally prays with truth. When all you can manage is, "Lord, please... just be with me," heaven bends down to listen.

It is easy to forget that Jesus Himself prayed this way. We often imagine Him praying with divine composure, but the Gospels show something far more human and far more comforting. In Gethsemane, He does not pray a long speech. He falls to the ground. He trembles. He repeats the same few words. He asks if the cup might pass. He feels sorrow press so hard upon Him that His sweat becomes like drops of blood. This is not distant perfection. This is God entering the very place where you pray today: a place of exhaustion, fear, and profound dependence. If Jesus prayed His deepest prayer in weakness, then your weakness does not disqualify your prayer. It unites it to His.

Prayer begins to change in suffering, not because God changes but because you do. When life narrows and the body weakens, the soul begins to see what matters. You no longer pray out of routine. You no longer pray to fulfill an obligation. You pray because something inside you knows that without God, you simply cannot face what is ahead. Illness strips away noise and leaves the essential truth uncovered: you belong to God, and you need Him. Not as an idea. Not as a religious concept. As a Father. As a Savior. As the One who holds every breath.

Many people fear that they do not pray "correctly," especially when suffering makes it difficult to concentrate. But prayer is not about technique. Prayer is about truth. You are not praying to impress a distant deity. You are speaking to the One who carries you. A child who climbs into her father's arms is not performing a ritual; she is seeking refuge. Suffering returns the soul to childhood in the holiest way. You find yourself whispering simple petitions: "Stay with me." "Give me strength." "I am scared." "Help." And these prayers—so short, so fragile—are more pleasing to God than the longest prayers spoken from comfort. He loves the voice that trembles, the voice that breaks, the voice that barely escapes the lips. He loves it because it trusts Him.

One of the greatest lies the enemy whispers during illness is this: "God is not listening to you anymore." But Scripture shatters that lie completely. The psalmist says God keeps your tears in His bottle—not your words, your tears. Christ says not a sparrow falls without the Father's care; how much more does the Father watch over a suffering child? St. Paul says the Spirit Himself prays inside you when you cannot form the words. The Spirit does not wait for your strength; He intercedes with groanings deeper than speech. When your heart aches so deeply you cannot speak, God hears the ache itself. When you lie awake at night, unable to sleep, staring at a ceiling that feels too quiet, God does not wait for you to begin praying. He is already present, already attentive, already listening to the wordless movements of your heart. Prayer in suffering is not about lifting yourself to God. It is about allowing God to descend into your weakness.

The truth is that you do not pray alone, especially now. Every time you whisper "Jesus," heaven responds. Every time you sigh in fear, Christ receives it as a prayer. Every time your body feels too tired to kneel or sit upright or even keep your thoughts steady, your weakness becomes the place where God does His most hidden work. Illness forces you to let go of the idea that prayer depends on your control. And that letting go is painful at first. But slowly, gently, it becomes liberating. You discover that God was never asking you to be strong. He was asking you to be His.

When you pray in weakness, God strengthens you in ways you cannot yet see. He does not always change the circumstances, but He changes the soul. He steadies parts of the heart you did not know were shaking. He quiets fears you could not name. He places courage in places where yesterday you felt only despair. These changes often happen so quietly that you only realize them later—when you notice that something inside you is no longer collapsing but standing. In Scripture, Elijah wanted to die under a broom tree, convinced he could not go on. What does God do? He sends an angel to touch him gently and say, "Arise and eat." Sometimes prayer in illness is not a mountaintop; it is God giving just enough strength for the next step, the next hour, the next breath.

But prayer is not only God's work in you; it is your heart's response to Him. Even the smallest act of turning toward God in weakness is a profound act of faith. When you whisper His name in fear, you are choosing trust over despair. When you ask for help in a hospital room, you are declaring that suffering does not have the final word. When you open your eyes in the morning and simply say, "Lord… be with me today," you are placing your life into the hands that shaped the stars. There is nothing small about that. Heaven hears such prayers with a joy you cannot imagine.

And because God knows how weak you feel, He does not ask you to carry more than you can. Breath prayers—just one line spoken slowly with your breathing—become holy in His sight: "Jesus, stay with me." "Lord, give me peace." "Into Your hands." "My strength is in You." A single verse of a psalm becomes a fortress: "The Lord is my light." "When I am afraid, I trust in You." "You are with me." Even closing your eyes and resting in silence becomes prayer, because prayer is not about speaking to God; prayer is about being with Him. St. Teresa of Avila said, "Prayer is nothing more than being with the One who loves us." Illness makes that sentence shine.

And so prayer begins to take on a new shape in your life. It becomes quieter, slower, more intimate. It is no longer measured by minutes or methods but by honesty. You may find that your deepest prayer happens not when you sit upright with a rosary in your hand, but when you lie still beneath a blanket, unable to do anything more than breathe God's name. You may discover that the prayers you thought were too weak to matter are the very ones God treasures most. You may realize that prayer in suffering is not about rising above weakness, but about letting God meet you within it. The prayer that says, "I cannot do this alone," is the prayer that allows God to be God. The prayer that says, "Stay with me," is the prayer that welcomes Christ into the centre of your fear. The prayer that says nothing at all—because the heart is too tired—becomes a prayer when you simply turn your thoughts, however faintly, toward the One who loves you.

In this season of illness, your soul is learning something profound: God desires your presence, not your performance. He is moved not by the strength of your voice but by the truth of your need. Jesus said, "Come to Me, all you who labour and are heavy laden, and I will give you rest." He did not say, "Come to Me with strong prayers," but simply, "Come." Cancer has taken much from you—energy, routine, predictability—but it has not taken your ability to come to God. Even if your coming is only a whisper, it is enough. Even if all you bring Him is your exhaustion, He receives it as an offering. Even if the only prayer you pray is, "Help me," heaven opens to hear it.

Prayer now becomes less about what you say to God and more about who God becomes for you. He becomes your steadiness when your mind races. He becomes your comfort when your body aches. He becomes your companion when the hours stretch long. He becomes your safe place when everything else feels fragile. And slowly, prayer becomes not something you do at certain times, but something you live. You pray in waiting rooms with your hands folded in your lap. You pray in treatment chairs with your eyes closed. You pray in the car as someone drives you home. You pray in the late hours of the night when sleep refuses to come. You pray in the silence when fear rises. You pray with a sigh, a breath, a tear—each one a kind of prayer God understands more deeply than words.

There will be moments when prayer feels dry, empty, or pointless. You may say to yourself, "I do not feel anything when I pray." But prayer is not about feeling. Prayer is about surrender. When you pray without feeling anything in return, you are offering God a deeper trust than you know. You are saying, in effect, "Even without comfort, even without certainty, I will turn to You." That is the prayer of the saints. That is the prayer of Christ Himself on the Cross. Feeling God's presence is a gift, but trusting Him without feeling is love.

And when you cannot pray at all, when the fatigue is too heavy or the anxiety too sharp, God does not step back. Instead, He steps forward. He surrounds you with people who pray for you, who lift your name to heaven when you cannot lift it yourself. He prompts the Church to intercede. He unites you to the communion of saints. He places your life within the Mass, where Christ forever intercedes for His people. He lets the Spirit groan within you with prayers too deep for words. Your silence does not end your prayer. Your silence becomes prayer. You are not praying alone. You have never prayed alone, not even once.

If you could see what happens in your soul every time you turn toward God in weakness, you would be overwhelmed with hope. You would see courage being planted like a seed. You would see fear slowly losing its grip. You would see God strengthening you in ways you do not yet understand. You would see heaven bending toward you. You would see Christ beside your bed, praying with you, praying for you, holding your prayer within His own. This is the mystery at the heart of suffering: when your strength fails, God's strength begins. When your voice trembles, His voice rises. When your prayer feels small, His mercy makes it great.

And so you do not need long prayers now. You do not need complicated words. You do not need perfect concentration. You need only to let your heart open—even slightly—to the God who loves you. Whisper His name. Breathe in His peace. Let your eyes close and know He is near. Say, "Jesus, stay with me," and trust that He will. Say, "Lord, have mercy," and trust that He hears. Say nothing at all, and trust that your very existence in His presence is a prayer.

You may think your suffering has weakened your spiritual life. In reality, it has made it real. It has taken prayer from the head to the heart. It has taken prayer from effort to surrender. It has taken prayer from routine to relationship. This chapter is not merely about learning how to pray when tired; it is about discovering what prayer truly is: the soul leaning on God when everything else feels too heavy.

Your body may be tired. Your mind may be weary. Your days may be filled with uncertainty. But your prayer—your simple, fragile, trembling prayer—is precious to God. It rises before Him like incense. It reaches Christ like a whisper reaches a friend sitting beside your bed. It draws the Spirit into the depths of your heart. It makes heaven nearer than your breath.

When strength fades, prayer begins. Not because you have finally learned how to pray, but because you have finally learned how to lean. And the God you lean on will not let you fall.

Seven

When God Feels Silent

There are seasons in the life of faith when God feels wonderfully near, when prayer seems to rise from the heart almost without effort, when Scripture feels alive and every word of worship glows with meaning. But there are other seasons, quieter and far more difficult, when heaven seems to close its doors, when prayers return to you like echoes, when the silence of God becomes almost more painful than the suffering itself. In the journey through cancer, that silence can appear suddenly and without warning. You may begin with a strong desire to pray, or you may cling to God instinctively in the early days of fear, but then something happens—days pass, fatigue deepens, the treatments drain your strength, and your prayer seems to meet only quiet. You lie awake at night and whisper His name, and nothing stirs. You reach for God in the early morning hours, and He feels far away. You ask, "Lord, where are You?" and the heavens do not part. You listen for the comforting voice you knew so well before illness, but now there is only stillness. It is a loneliness of the soul that no one else can fully understand.

Yet the silence of God, as painful and confusing as it feels, is not a sign of abandonment. Scripture gives us permission to say what you may have whispered in your heart: "How long, O Lord?" "Why do You hide Your face from me?" "My God, why have You forsaken me?" These are not the cries of unbelievers. They are the cries of people who know God so intimately that they cannot bear His apparent absence. They are the prayers of those who believe fiercely enough to complain, those who love deeply enough to protest, those who trust enough to question. And the remarkable thing is that God placed these prayers in the Bible. He wanted them there so that you would know that the experience of His silence is not a spiritual failure but a spiritual inheritance. The saints walked this road long before you, and Christ Himself walked it most of all.

There is a mystery hidden within God's silence, and it is this: silence is not the absence of God. Silence is one of the ways God is present. We often mistake silence for distance because our emotions go quiet at the same time. But God is not governed by your feelings. His presence does not fluctuate with your senses. His love does not fade when your heart grows tired. Silence is not God stepping away; silence is God stepping into the deepest part of your soul, the part where words no longer serve and only love remains. Silence is God drawing you into a communion so profound that it cannot be expressed through sound.

Scripture reveals that silence is not the opposite of revelation—it is the preparation for it. Think of Elijah on the mountain. He had seen God's power before, had heard His voice, had confronted kings and prophets with fire in his bones. Yet on Mount Horeb, when he desperately needed God to speak, there came first a wind so strong it shattered rocks, then an earthquake, then a fire—yet the Lord was in none of these. Only after the tumult came the "still, small voice"—or as some translations say, "a sound of sheer silence." God was in the silence. Elijah had to stand in that quiet long enough to recognize that God was speaking in a way he had never heard before.

Israel learned the same truth in the desert. After the drama of the Red Sea and the miracles of Egypt, the people entered a landscape defined by quiet. No cities, no crowds, no noise. Only sand, sky, and silence. Yet it was in that silence that God fed them, guided them, shaped them, and taught them to trust Him. The desert is not the place where God disappears. It is the place where He prepares the heart to listen.

The prophets knew this silence too. During the long years of exile, when it seemed as though God had forsaken His people, Israel learned that the silence of God was not the cancellation of His promises but the deepening of them. Centuries passed without the voice of a prophet, yet during that silence God was setting the stage for the coming of His Son. Salvation history turns on the hinge of a God who works most powerfully when He works most quietly.

And then there is Holy Saturday—the most silent day in all of Christian faith. Christ has died. The disciples hide behind locked doors. Mary holds her grief in a heart that has never felt so empty. Heaven itself feels motionless. There is no answer, no comfort, no sign. It is the day God seems absent. Yet the ancient homily tells us what was really happening: "A great silence fell upon the earth, for the King slept." In that silence, Christ descended to the realm of death to break its gates from the inside. The world saw only stillness, but hell felt the shockwave of redemption. The silence of Holy Saturday was the hour of God's most hidden triumph.

This is the secret Scripture tries to teach us: when God seems silent, He is never still. His silence is not inactivity. His silence is intimacy. His silence is the slow, patient work of grace shaping your soul in ways you cannot yet perceive. You may feel nothing. You may fear that your prayers are going unheard. You may wonder if God has stepped away. But silence is often the evidence that God is closer than breath, drawing the soul into a trust deeper than understanding. God's silence is not God withholding Himself; it is God giving Himself in a form too profound for the senses.

And you must know this, especially now: Jesus Himself prayed into silence. In Gethsemane, He brought His fear and sorrow before the Father. He prayed, "Let this cup pass from Me." And what came back? No voice. No angelic reassurance. Only the quiet of the night. Yet Jesus trusted that the Father heard Him, even though His human heart received no comforting word. He prayed again. And again the silence remained. On the Cross, Jesus prayed the most haunting line in Scripture: "My God, My God, why have You forsaken Me?" These are not the words of a man who has lost faith. These are the words of a man holding onto the Father even when the Father's presence cannot be felt. Christ entered the silence so that you would never walk into your own alone.

That means something extraordinary: the silence you feel is not a sign that you've been abandoned. It is the place where your suffering touches the suffering of Christ. It is the place where Christ prays with you. It is the place where your heart meets His. God does not leave you in silence. He enters silence with you.

And so the silence you feel now is not a doorway closing but a deeper doorway opening. It invites you into the same trust that Jesus showed in Gethsemane, the same surrender He lived on the Cross, the same hope that waited in the quiet of the tomb. When God feels silent, He is not turning His face away. He is drawing you into the mystery of His own Son's prayer. The silence of God is not a barrier; it is a veil. And behind that veil, the Father is closer than He has ever been.

Yet for the soul in suffering, this silence can still feel unbearable. You want comfort; you want reassurance; you want to feel God wrap around you like a warm blanket. You want signs. You want consolations. You want something—anything—to answer back. But faith is not measured by the amount of comfort you receive. Faith is measured by the love that keeps reaching when comfort does not come. And that love is already in you. The fact that you continue to turn toward God in the quiet, even when you feel nothing, is itself the work of grace. You are not holding yourself together. God is holding you together, and the very desire to pray is proof that He has not withdrawn.

When your emotions go numb, when prayer feels flat, when Scripture feels distant, when Mass feels heavy, do not think that God has stepped aside. The numbness of the heart in suffering is not the absence of grace; it is often the sign that grace has moved deeper, beyond the surface of feelings, into the hidden places where courage and endurance are born. What you feel as emptiness is God making room for something new. Emotional dryness teaches the soul to trust God for God's sake, not for the feelings He sometimes gives. And trust that is born in silence is trust that nothing in the world can shake.

Sometimes the silence is God teaching you how to rely on Him rather than on the emotional consolations that once sustained you. Sometimes silence is God removing the things that distracted you, not to punish you, but to form you. Sometimes silence is simply what love looks like when God draws you closer. Think of a parent who sits beside a sick child through the night. They do not talk endlessly. They do not overwhelm the child with speeches. They remain, steady and quiet, their presence a comfort deeper than words. God's silence is like that. He is beside you with a love that does not need noise to be real.

In this quiet, prayer begins to take on a different character. You may find that long or eloquent prayers no longer rise from your lips. That is not failure. That is honesty. There is no need to pretend strength when you feel weak. Your prayer now might be a sentence, or half a sentence, or simply the name "Jesus." And that is enough. A whispered name from a suffering heart reaches God more swiftly than a thousand words spoken in comfort. The early Christians knew this; their simplest prayer was the one still prayed today: "Lord Jesus Christ, have mercy on me." When you breathe that prayer from a hospital bed, you join a chorus of saints who learned to trust God in silence.

There will be moments when you wonder if your prayer is doing anything at all. But you must understand that silence is not an unanswered prayer. Silence is an answered prayer in a different form. God is strengthening you in ways that do not announce themselves. He is forming patience, deepening faith, purifying love, humbling pride, teaching surrender, and making your soul more spacious for His presence. These are not loud works. These are quiet works. They grow in the hidden soil of silence, like roots that strengthen a tree during winter. When spring comes, the tree blossoms. But the roots grew in the cold.

In your silence, God is growing roots in you.

And though you may not feel it now, you will one day discover that something within you has changed—that you trust God more deeply than before, that you fear death less, that you cling to hope more fiercely, that you love more tenderly, that you endure more peacefully. None of those graces appear with fanfare. They appear like dawn: gently, inevitably, silently. God is forming the dawn in you even now.

If you want to know how to pray in this silence, it is simple: pray honestly. Tell God, "I cannot feel You right now." Tell Him, "I miss Your voice." Tell Him, "I need You to hold me." Tell Him, "I am afraid You are far away." He is not offended by these words. He is moved by them. Prayer is not pretending. Prayer is being known. The Psalms teach this again and again. God desires truth in the inward heart, and truth in suffering often sounds like longing, confusion, or desperation. These prayers are not less holy; they are more holy, because they are real.

And if all you can manage is silence itself, then let that silence be your prayer. Turn your heart toward heaven—even briefly—and God will receive that turning as a full prayer. The great spiritual writers speak of a form of prayer called "resting in God," a prayer where no words are spoken, and no feelings rise, and yet the soul remains quietly in God's presence. You can rest in God even when you cannot think of Him clearly. You can rest in God even when fear interrupts every thought. You can rest in God when you lie down too tired to speak. Rest is prayer when the heart intends it.

The silence of God is not meant to break you but to sanctify you. It is not meant to frighten you but to deepen your trust. It is not meant to distance you but to draw you closer. In the silence, God is teaching you how to lean on Him in a way you never have before. He is making your faith more resilient, more interior, more unshakeable. He is teaching you to find Him not only in light but in shadow, not only in joy but in sorrow, not only when He speaks but when He seems still. And faith learned in silence becomes faith that darkness cannot overcome.

If you could see what God is doing in this silence, you would never fear it again. You would see Him strengthening your soul gently, almost imperceptibly, shaping virtues in you that will endure into eternity. You would see the Father watching over you with tender vigilance. You would see Christ praying with you, carrying your heart in His own. You would see the Spirit breathing in you, sustaining you when your strength fades. You would see that not one moment of this silence is wasted.

So when God feels silent, do not conclude He has stepped away. Conclude He is nearer than ever. When He does not answer in the ways you expect, conclude He is answering in ways too deep for you to grasp right now. When your heart feels numb, conclude that God is operating at depths beyond emotion. When you cannot feel His love, choose to believe His promises, for His promises are truer than your feelings.

The silence of God is not the end of your prayer life. It is the doorway into a new one. A quieter one. A deeper one. A holier one. A prayer not built on emotion but on trust. A prayer not fashioned from strength but from surrender. A prayer that does not rise because you feel God, but because you need Him. That need is your offering. That offering is your prayer. And God receives it with more love than you can imagine.

In this silence, you are held. In this silence, you are formed. In this silence, God is working. And one day, when the silence lifts, you will discover that the God you feared had withdrawn was the God who was carrying you all along.

Eight

Held Up by the Prayers of Others

There are moments in the journey of illness when prayer feels like lifting a weight you simply cannot move. You try to speak to God, but the words will not rise. Your mind drifts, your heart feels flat, and your body is too tired to do anything more than breathe. You may lie in bed and whisper a few words, only to feel them fall back toward you like leaves dropped in still air. You may want to pray—truly want to—but wanting no longer translates into doing. And in those moments, a quiet worry can begin to form: "What happens if I can't pray anymore? Will God leave me? Will I drift away? Will my faith disappear along with my strength?" It is an honest fear, and a painful one, especially for someone who has loved God, spoken with Him, trusted Him, leaned on Him. It feels like losing something precious. Yet the truth hidden within Scripture and woven through every page of salvation history is this: God never intended anyone to pray alone. He never placed the whole weight of prayer upon a single pair of shoulders. He built the people of God so that when one member suffers, the others carry them; when one voice falls silent, the others rise; when one heart grows weary, another heart beats for them. You were never meant to sustain your spiritual life by yourself. You were meant to be held.

This truth runs through the entire biblical story like a golden thread. Prayer is never portrayed as the solitary achievement of a heroic individual. Even when the saints pray alone, they pray as part of a people, wrapped in the prayers of others, shaped by the intercession that surrounds them like air. When Moses grew too tired to lift his hands in battle, God did not ask him to force himself into superhuman strength. Instead, Aaron and Hur came beside him, one on each side, and held up his arms. The victory belonged to God, but it came through the strength of the community supporting the exhausted man at its centre. The Scripture does not say Moses failed. The Scripture says Israel prevailed because others lifted what he no longer could. Your life is meant to be held the same way. God does not look at your weakness and say, "Try harder." He looks at your weakness and sends people to your side.

Think of the paralytic in the Gospel, a man who could not walk, could not stand, could not carry himself to Jesus. If salvation depended on his strength, he never would have reached the Lord. But he had friends—four of them—who refused to give up. They carried him through the streets, lifted him onto a roof, broke through the ceiling, and lowered him down right in front of Christ. And Scripture says something remarkable: "When Jesus saw their faith, He said to the paralytic, 'Your sins are forgiven.'" Not his faith alone. Theirs. The faith of others became the doorway of healing for a man who could not reach Jesus by his own effort. When you cannot pray, when you cannot lift yourself to God, the prayers of others become the roof-breaking strength that brings you before Christ. Their faith surrounds you. Their voices speak when yours cannot. Their hope carries you into the presence of the One who heals.

This pattern appears again in the Acts of the Apostles, when Peter is imprisoned by King Herod. The situation seems hopeless. Chains bind him, soldiers guard him, the night is dark, and there is no plan. But Scripture records one quiet detail: "The Church prayed fervently for him." They gathered in homes, in small rooms, in hidden spaces, lifting his name to heaven. Peter himself was asleep, helpless, silent, unable to act or pray with clarity. But the Church prayed. And in the middle of the night an angel of the Lord came, struck his chains off, led him past the guards, and brought him safely out into the street. Peter later confessed he had not even realized what God was doing until he was already free. This is the astonishing power of intercession: God was answering prayers Peter did not have the strength to pray for himself. The Church carried him. The Body lifted the burden the individual could not bear. When illness renders you too weary to ask for help, God hears the prayers prayed in the voices of those who love you.

It is important to understand what this means for your own suffering. When cancer limits your strength, when anxiety steals your focus, when medications fog your thoughts, when pain turns your mind inward, you are not expected to pray with the clarity or intensity you once had. God does not measure your prayer by your output. God measures your prayer by your belonging. And you belong to a Body—a mystical Body—whose prayers do not depend on your strength. The Church prays for you. The Mass is offered for you. The saints intercede for you without ceasing. The Blessed Mother carries your name before her Son with a tenderness that never tires. Your loved ones, even those who do not know how to express it perfectly, whisper your name to heaven in ways that reach the heart of God. You are surrounded by intercession like a warm mantle, even when you feel too weak to add your own voice.

Often, people feel embarrassed to let others pray for them. They feel like a burden. They feel like they should be stronger, more composed, more spiritually anchored. But letting others pray for you is not a burden—it is a blessing. It is not a failure—it is faith. It is an act of humility that acknowledges the truth: none of us were made to walk this road alone. The early Church understood this so deeply that St. Paul wrote, "If one member suffers, all suffer together; if one is honoured, all rejoice together." He did not say, "If one suffers, the others cheer from afar." He said the suffering of one becomes the prayer of all. Your weakness makes the Body of Christ move toward you, not away from you. Your vulnerability invites love. And that love, when lifted in prayer, becomes a kind of spiritual shelter.

Sometimes, the help others offer will come in the form of spoken prayer—hands laid gently upon you, a whispered blessing, a rosary said in your name. Sometimes it will come through service—rides to appointments, meals cooked, messages sent, kindness offered. Sometimes it will come through the sacraments—through the priest who brings you the Eucharist when you cannot attend Mass, through the anointing that strengthens your soul, through the confessions that lighten your heart. And sometimes it will come in ways that remain unseen on earth but radiant in heaven—the saints interceding, the angels guarding, the souls in glory praying with a fire of love you cannot yet fathom. God sends these helpers not because you are weak, but because you are loved.

And your "yes," however small, allows this communion to unfold. When you say, even silently, "I cannot do this alone," heaven hears an invitation. When you allow others to pray for you, you allow God to act through them. When you accept help, you open the door for grace to enter through the hearts of those who love you. You do not need to be strong enough. You do not need eloquent prayers. You do not need to perform faith. Your task is simply to allow yourself to be held.

There is a sacred humility in letting yourself be carried, a humility that mirrors the very heart of Christ, who allowed Simon of Cyrene to help Him carry His Cross. Jesus, who could command storms and raise the dead, permitted another man to shoulder His burden for a few steps. He did not refuse the help. He did not insist on walking alone. He let someone else's strength become part of His own journey. This moment in the Passion is not an accident; it is a revelation. When you accept the prayers and help of others, you are not stepping away from Christ—you are imitating Him. You are allowing the Father to send you a Simon in your hour of need. And the grace flowing through that acceptance is greater than any prayer you could force from a place of exhaustion.

There is something mysterious and beautiful about the way God weaves the lives of His children together. When you cannot pray, others do. When you cannot lift your spirit, others lift it for you. When your mind is clouded by worry or medication or pain, the clarity of someone else's love becomes the clarity of your prayer. You may not feel anything happening, but heaven is moving because people are speaking your name before God. A mother prays for her child. A friend lights a candle. A priest remembers you at the altar. A stranger at Mass offers up their suffering for someone who is ill without knowing it is you. In ways hidden from your eyes, your life is being lifted upward on currents of prayer you did not generate. This is what it means to belong to Christ's Body: the strength of one covers the weakness of another.

And beyond this earthly communion stands the vast communion of saints—a great cloud of witnesses who intercede ceaselessly for the children of God. They do not grow tired. They do not forget. They do not become distracted. Their intercession surrounds you like a mantle of fire and tenderness. The saints pray for your healing, your courage, your peace, your perseverance. Mary, the Mother of God, prays for you with a love immeasurably more gentle than even the best earthly mother. She sees your tears. She understands your fear. She carries your sufferings to her Son, who receives her prayers with the affection only a son can give. Your loved ones who have gone before you pray for you as well, not vaguely or distantly, but personally and passionately. There is not a single moment of your suffering that passes without heaven noticing it, loving you through it, and lifting you in prayer.

So when you sit in silence and cannot form the words, you are not alone. When you lie awake at two in the morning and feel unable to pray, know that someone, somewhere, is praying for you at that very hour. When you feel too tired to open your Bible or too numb to say "Lord," the Holy Spirit Himself is praying in you with groanings too deep for words. Your soul is never without prayer, even when your lips fall silent. The current of intercession that surrounds you does not depend on your strength. It depends on God's faithfulness—and His faithfulness never falters.

If you could see with spiritual sight what is happening around you, even at this very moment, your heart would be flooded with peace. You would see angels standing guard beside your bed. You would see saints leaning toward you with compassion. You would see the prayers of friends rising like incense before the throne of God. You would see Christ holding your heart within His own wounds and offering your suffering to the Father with infinite love. You would see that you are wrapped in a communion that is larger, stronger, and more enduring than any illness. This communion is the very life of the Church, and it exists for your sake, especially now, when you feel weakest.

Your part in all of this is simple. You are not asked to pray with eloquence or strength. You are not asked to muster energy you do not have. You are not asked to feel spiritual. You are asked only to let yourself be loved. You are asked to say yes—however faintly—to the God who has surrounded you with so many hearts willing to intercede for you. That yes does not need to be loud. It does not need to be confident. It can be tired, whispered, shaky, or even wordless. God hears the yes of the heart long before the tongue finds the courage to voice it.

Your small yes makes space for grace to flow. It allows others to become Christ to you. It allows the Church to carry you. It allows the saints to surround you. It allows the Holy Spirit to pray within you. And it allows your suffering—not your strength—to become the place where God reveals the unimaginable depth of His love.

You may feel that you are doing nothing right now. But in God's eyes, you are doing something profoundly holy: you are letting yourself be held. And the God who holds you through the hands and voices of others will not let you fall.

Nine

The Long Nights: God in the Hours When Hope Feels Thin

There is a particular kind of suffering that only appears at night, a heaviness that waits for the house to grow quiet before it settles over the heart. During the day there are voices, appointments, routines, conversations, distractions—small mercies that keep the heart from turning inward too sharply. But when the sun goes down and the rooms darken and the noise fades and sleep refuses to come, the soul finds itself alone with thoughts that do not rise during the warmth of daylight. Every fear grows sharper. Every worry speaks louder. The mind imagines futures that may never come to pass, yet still they feel real in the darkness. Illness always feels heavier at night. Pain feels deeper. Exhaustion feels more complete. The quiet of the world amplifies the noise inside your own heart. This is the hour when hope feels thin, when faith feels fragile, when the presence of God feels distant, even though it is not. And yet it is within these long, restless hours that the mystery of God's tenderness often reveals itself most quietly.

Night has always been the testing ground of the soul. Scripture speaks of this again and again, not to frighten but to prepare. Jacob wrestles the angel in the dark. Samuel hears the voice of God in the early hours before dawn. The psalmist keeps watch through the night, speaking to God from his bed in whispers shaped by fear and longing. Jesus Himself chooses the night for His final agony—the night in Gethsemane, the night when His friends slept and He remained awake in sorrow. These stories are not incidental. They reveal that night exposes the truth of our hearts in a way daylight never could. At night we discover our limits, our fears, our doubts, our longing for God. But we also discover that God is not put off by our fragility; He draws near to it. He enters the hours that frighten us most.

Anyone who has walked through illness knows the way pain intensifies once the world goes quiet. Doctors will tell you that the body's chemistry shifts after midnight, making symptoms seem sharper and endurance feel thinner. Psychologists will tell you that the imagination becomes more active when the external world grows still, which is why anxieties flourish more quickly at three in the morning than they do at three in the afternoon. Spiritual writers will tell you that the night has always been a crucible—a place where the soul, stripped of distraction and comfort, confronts the rawness of its need for God. None of this means you are weak or failing or losing faith when the night becomes difficult. It simply means you are human, and you are not the first to walk this path. Even saints cried into the darkness and begged God for comfort they could not feel. Even Jesus, the Son of God, stayed awake in fear while the world slept. If He entered these hours, you can be sure He is present in yours.

The Gethsemane of your life is not a metaphor; it is a reality. Every night when you lie awake with thoughts racing or pain pulsing or fear whispering that tomorrow will be too heavy, you are standing in the garden with Christ. He is not asleep. He is not far away. He is awake in your sorrow long before you are. The Gospel of Matthew tells us that He prayed three times, and each time He returned to find His closest friends sleeping. They loved Him, yet they could not stay awake with Him. They wanted to support Him, yet their bodies gave out. He knew the loneliness of carrying a burden no one else fully understood. He knew the sting of suffering in the darkness with no human companionship. And because He entered that loneliness, He transformed it. Now, every believer who suffers in the night keeps vigil not alone, but beside the God who chose to suffer sleeplessness for love of us.

When night comes and sleep does not, a strange silence descends. It is easy to assume that silence means absence, that God should feel close but does not, that prayer should bring comfort but instead feels empty. But silence is not the opposite of God's presence. Silence is often the form God's presence takes when the heart is too burdened to feel anything at all. This is why the psalmist can say, "On my bed I remember You; on You I muse through the watches of the night" (Psalm 63). The psalmist does not wait until morning to pray. He discovers God in the very hour when prayer feels least possible. And he discovers that God is not found by emotion, but by remembrance—by the quiet act of turning the soul toward Him even when the soul feels numb.

There is a beautiful truth hidden in the heart of nighttime suffering: you are never the only one awake. You may look around your darkened room and see nothing but shadows, but heaven does not sleep. Psalm 121 declares, "He who keeps Israel neither slumbers nor sleeps." This means that while you lie awake staring at the ceiling, while you clutch your blanket in fear or discomfort, while you take slow breaths to calm a racing heart, God is keeping vigil over you. He is as alert at midnight as He is at noon. Your sleeplessness does not exhaust Him. Your fears do not overwhelm Him. Your tears do not confuse Him. He is present, steady, awake. The silence of your room is not the silence of God. His watchful love fills every corner of the night even when your senses cannot feel it.

It may not feel like this. Feelings often disappear at night. The exhaustion of the body, the racing of the mind, the dim light of the room—all of these dull spiritual sensitivity. The heart becomes less receptive. Emotions flatten. It is normal in these hours to feel cut off from God, not because He has moved away, but because the soul has reached the limits of its own strength. In the daytime, faith often feels more natural because our senses cooperate with us—sunlight warms the room, conversation lifts the spirit, routine provides stability. But night removes these supports, and faith must walk more quietly, more slowly, more simply. Nighttime faith is not emotional faith; it is covenant faith. It rests not on what you feel, but on who God is.

There is a reason the Christian tradition places so much weight on God's fidelity rather than our perception. If God's presence depended on our ability to feel it, then our darkest nights would be proof of His absence. But God's presence is grounded not in our strength but in His promise. "I am with you always," Jesus says—not "I am with you always when you feel Me," but simply "always." The covenant God keeps watch when your eyes cannot. The faithful God remains steady when your emotions fail. The God who neither slumbers nor sleeps holds your life in His hands when all you can do is lie awake and breathe.

If you have ever looked at the clock and seen the hours crawl—12:47 a.m., 1:19 a.m., 2:02 a.m.—you know the peculiar loneliness of the night. Hospital rooms intensify this. The hum of machines, the pale light from the hallway, the uncomfortable bed, the sterile smell, the long quiet stretches when nurses walk by with soft footsteps but no one enters your room—these moments test the soul more than any theology class could ever prepare you for. But it is often in these moments, when words fail and prayer becomes nothing more than a whispered, "Lord, stay with me," that grace works most deeply. Because prayer at night is not about eloquence. It is not about long devotions. It is not about strength at all. Prayer at night is a reaching—sometimes weak, sometimes desperate, sometimes barely conscious—toward the God who is already reaching toward you.

There is a kind of prayer that only suffering can teach, a kind of prayer that emerges when you no longer have the energy or clarity to pray as you once did. It is a prayer of presence rather than performance. A prayer of surrender rather than striving. A prayer that simply says, "Here I am, Lord," without any adornment. And this prayer, offered in weakness, is often more powerful than the most beautiful prayers spoken in times of peace. St. Paul writes that "the Spirit intercedes with sighs too deep for words" (Romans 8:26). This is not poetry; it is theology. When you lie awake unable to form sentences, the Holy Spirit Himself prays in you. Your weakness does not impede prayer; it becomes the very place where divine prayer takes root.

When fear rises in the darkness, sometimes the most honest prayer you can offer is a breath. To inhale slowly and say the name of Jesus in your heart is itself a profound act of faith. To whisper, "Be near," is a prayer the angels carry immediately to the throne of God. To recite a fragment of Scripture—"The Lord is my light," "Into Your hands," "You are with me"—is to anchor your heart to truth when your emotions cannot. And when you are too tired even for that, to stay still and let God look at you is enough. The saints called this resting prayer: allowing yourself to be held by God without effort or words.

But the night also carries temptations. Despair often whispers loudest at three in the morning. The mind murmurs dark predictions about the future, magnifies uncertainties, imagines worst-case scenarios, repeats questions for which there are no immediate answers. Thoughts formed in these hours are rarely trustworthy. The Christian tradition understands this. Monks of the early Church wrote about the "noonday devil," but they also wrote about the "night-watch battle"—the spiritual vulnerability that comes with exhaustion. Which means that when your thoughts feel heavy and hopeless in the dark, you are not sinning. You are not losing faith. You are simply facing what countless believers before you have faced. And just as they were not alone, neither are you.

There is a reason the Church gives us psalms that sound like cries in the dark. "Why are You so far from my groaning?" "My tears have been my food day and night." "Out of the depths I cry to You, O Lord." These words are not the prayers of people who felt spiritually triumphant. They are the prayers of people who lay awake with pounding hearts and trembling thoughts, people who wondered whether morning would ever come. God preserved these prayers in Scripture so that you would know that He is not scandalized by your nighttime fears. He takes them seriously. He receives them with tenderness. He hears every whisper you offer in the long hours when your strength thins out and your courage feels spent.

You may notice something else in Scripture: some of God's greatest works happen while His people are sleeping or suffering in the dark. Israel crossed the Red Sea in the night. Samuel heard God's voice before dawn. Christ was born while the world slept. The Resurrection—upon which the entire universe turns—happened quietly, invisibly, in the stillness before sunrise. God often chooses the night to reshape the world. And that means the night of your suffering is not wasted time. It is not a void where nothing happens. It is the workshop of God. He is doing something in you, even when you cannot sense it. He is strengthening what feels weak, softening what has hardened, deepening what feels shallow, preparing your heart to receive grace in ways it could not have received in the busyness of the day.

Even when you feel abandoned in the night, Christ is nearest. There is an ancient Christian insight, repeated by the Fathers and the mystics: when God feels distant, He is often closer than ever, because He is working in places too deep for your emotions to reach. Emotions operate on the surface of consciousness. God works in the depths. And illness—especially illness endured at night—forces the soul into those depths, into the quiet interior place where God speaks without sound. The silence that frightens you is not the silence of emptiness; it is the silence of mystery, the silence of a God who communicates not with thunder but with presence.

When despair knocks in the darkness, you are not required to defeat it with argument. You can simply turn your face—however weakly—toward the God who watches over you. If you can say the name of Jesus, even once, even silently, you have already placed yourself in His protection. If you cannot even say His name, if your heart feels numb or exhausted or overwhelmed, He comes to stand beside you anyway. He does not wait for you to feel ready. He does not wait for your courage to return. He does not demand that you pray eloquently or triumphantly. He asks only for permission to be near, and even that permission can be nothing more than a weary sigh that says, "Lord…stay."

There is a tenderness in Christ's heart for those who suffer in the night. He who sweat blood under the olive trees does not forget the agony of sleepless sorrow. He who begged His friends to stay awake with Him knows the ache of hoping for comfort that does not arrive. He who watched the torches approaching in the darkness understands what it means to wait for news, for results, for relief. Because He has lived your night, He can sanctify it. Because He has endured your fear, He can calm it. Because He has kept vigil for you, you are never keeping vigil alone.

And so, when morning finally breaks and daylight moves across the floor of your room, you may feel as though you survived something enormous. You may feel tired, wrung out, emotionally thin. But do not underestimate what happened in those hours. God was not absent. He was sustaining you breath by breath. He was praying in you with sighs too deep for words. He was holding together your mind and heart when you felt they might unravel. He was planting seeds of grace that will bear fruit in ways you may not yet see. What feels like barely surviving may in fact be the quiet victory of grace.

Long nights can change the soul. They refine it. They teach a person that dependence is not weakness. They strip away pretences and reveal the simple truth that every human being is held in existence by a love stronger than illness, stronger than fear, stronger than death itself. And once this truth reveals itself, even dimly, the night loses some of its terror. You still feel the heaviness, the discomfort, the weariness—but you begin to sense that the night is not empty. You begin to suspect that Someone is awake with you. You begin to trust that you are watched over by eyes that never close.

If you could see the spiritual reality of your room at night, you would never fear being alone again. You would see Christ seated beside your bed, not watching from a distance but leaning close enough to hear every breath. You would see angels standing guard, protecting you with vigilance far stronger than your anxiety. You would see saints interceding for you, their love burning brighter than the darkness that frightens you. You would see that heaven is nearer than the shadows on your wall. But faith invites you to trust these realities even when you cannot see them, because God's promises do not depend on your vision—they depend on His fidelity.

And so the night becomes not a place of abandonment but a strange kind of sanctuary. A place where hope is tested and purified. A place where prayer becomes simpler and more honest. A place where the soul learns to lean on God not because it feels strong, but because it has nothing else to lean on. A place where Christ keeps vigil so faithfully that the darkness becomes thin with His presence.

When the next long night comes—and it will—you may still feel fear. You may still feel restless. You may still struggle to sleep. But you will not enter it alone. The God who neither slumbers nor sleeps will be watching over you. The Christ who stayed awake in His own anguish will be awake with you. The Spirit who intercedes for you will be praying within you. The saints will be whispering your name before the throne of God. And even if you feel nothing but exhaustion, the truth will remain unchanged: the night belongs not to fear, not to despair, not to illness, but to the God who fills every hour with His unbreakable love.

If all you can do is whisper, "Stay with me," that is enough. If you cannot even whisper, your very breath becomes prayer. Christ understands. Christ remains. Christ keeps watch. And the light that seems distant will come, just as it always does, because no night—no matter how long—can overcome the dawn that God Himself has promised

Ten

When the Night Gives Way to the First Light of Hope

There comes a point in the journey through suffering when the darkness, though still present, begins to soften at the edges. Not because pain has lifted. Not because answers have come. Not because the fear has vanished. It happens for a quieter reason: the soul has learned—slowly, painfully, almost imperceptibly—that God did not leave when you passed through the valley, nor when the silence stretched, nor when the nights grew long. Part II walked through the weariness of prayer, the bewilderment of God's silence, the gift of being carried by others, and the harsh hours when sleep refused to come. None of these moments were small. They stripped away illusions, exposed the fragility of the human heart, and made space for a deeper kind of knowing: the knowing that God remains even when you cannot feel Him.

And now you stand again at a threshold. Not the threshold of fear and confusion that marked the beginning of suffering, but a different one—a threshold where the soul begins to recognize the hidden work

God has been doing beneath the surface of your exhaustion. You have prayed when you had no words. You have endured silence without assuming abandonment. You have let the Church lift you when you could not lift yourself. You have survived nights that felt endless. These are not simply episodes of suffering; they are forms of grace. Something has been happening within you, even as everything around you seemed still. God has been shaping your heart to see differently. Not with naïve eyes. Not with escapism. But with the eyes of someone who has met God in the dark and therefore is able, at last, to discern the faint outline of dawn.

If Part II revealed anything, it is that prayer in weakness is not a lesser prayer—it is the truest kind. It is the prayer of Gethsemane. It is the prayer of Christ Himself. And when you pray in weakness, you unknowingly enter into the very strength of God. That strength does not take the form of sudden emotional relief or bursts of confidence. It takes the form of endurance, of quiet faithfulness, of a heart that keeps turning toward God even when no consolation comes. This is not the faith of the untested. It is the faith of the crucified and risen Christ taking root in you.

Suffering alters the way the soul listens. It removes the noise that once drowned out the deeper voice of God. It exposes longings you did not know you carried. It teaches you that God is not only the God of miracles but the God of watches-in-the-night, the God who leans close when words fail, the God who binds the heart to Himself not by removing pain but by remaining faithful in the midst of it. And because you have now tasted that fidelity in the night, you are capable of hearing something that could not have been spoken earlier: that suffering has not disqualified you from hope—it has prepared you for it.

Hope is not born in moments of triumph. It is born in moments of truth. It arises when the soul discovers that God is present not only in healing but also in the very ache that longs for healing. It is born when you realize that the darkness did not destroy you, nor did it separate you from the One who held you through every hour. Hope grows when the heart understands that even if the path remains steep, it is not empty. It is filled with the footprints of the One who has been leading you quietly, step by step, through terrain you never wanted to walk.

And now, because of everything you have endured, you are ready to hear that hope is not the same as optimism. Optimism depends on circumstances. Hope depends on God. Optimism rises and falls with outcomes. Hope stands firm because Christ stands firm. Optimism asks for good news. Hope anchors itself in the Good News already given: the Resurrection, the promise that death does not have the last word, the assurance that no suffering—no matter how long or how deep—can outlast the love of God.

Nothing in your circumstances may have changed. The diagnosis may remain. The treatment may continue. The nights may still be difficult. Yet something within you has shifted. You have learned that prayer can survive exhaustion. You have seen that God's silence is not God's absence. You have been held by the prayers of those who love you. You have discovered that the night is not godless; it is the hour in which God keeps watch with a tenderness you did not expect. And now these truths gather like quiet lights on the horizon, preparing you for the next movement in this journey: the movement toward hope that does not lie.

You are stepping into Part III not as someone who has conquered suffering but as someone who has encountered God within it. That encounter—hidden, fragile, often unnoticed—has already begun to reshape the landscape of your heart. You are ready, now, for the truths that only the wounded can understand: that Christian hope is stronger than fear, that your identity in God cannot be diminished by illness, that weakness can become a dwelling place for divine power, and that nothing offered to Christ in love is ever wasted.

The valley has not ended. The road is still long. But you do not walk it as the same person who entered it. You walk it with a heart that has learned—slowly, painfully, beautifully—that God does His best work in the dark, and that dawn always comes for those who keep their eyes—even tired, tearful eyes—turned toward Him.

When you are ready, we will take the next step. Hope is waiting there.

III

HOPE THAT DOES NOT LIE

Eleven

The Difference Between Optimism and Christian Hope

There comes a point in every season of illness when the heart grows tired of trying to stay positive. People around you say things like "Stay strong" or "Think good thoughts" or "Keep believing things will turn around," and you nod because you know they mean well, but inside you feel the weight of something deeper: this is not a situation you can simply "positive-think" your way out of. Optimism has its place, and sometimes it even gives a little burst of energy in the early days of treatment, but it cannot carry the soul through the valleys that illness uncovers. The soul needs something sturdier. Something that doesn't collapse when the news is not what you hoped for. Something that does not rise and fall with your energy, your emotions, or the latest scan. Something that holds you even when you cannot hold yourself. And that "something" is not optimism. It is hope.

Optimism is rooted in circumstances. It depends on the possibility that things might get better, that medicine will work, that the next round of tests will show improvement, that the fog of exhaustion will lift soon. It is a way of looking forward with a kind of emotional brightness, a confidence in probabilities or possibilities. And in the early moments of illness, it can seem like enough. You tell yourself, "Let's hope the numbers come down," "Let's hope the treatment responds," "Let's hope the side effects stay manageable." There is nothing wrong with this. In fact, it is natural. But as the journey deepens, you discover the limits of optimism. You discover that optimism cannot survive the nights when fear tightens around the heart. It cannot calm the anxiety of waiting for results that could reshape your future. It cannot hold you when tears fall silently and you wonder how much more your body and spirit can endure. Optimism is a fair-weather companion; it clings to hope only when the path looks clear.

Christian hope is of an entirely different substance. It does not grow out of circumstances but out of a Person. It does not depend on what might happen tomorrow but on what has already happened in Christ. It is not rooted in probabilities but in the unshakeable reality of the Resurrection. When Scripture speaks of hope, it is not speaking about a vague emotional positivity; it is speaking about a confidence that flows from the empty tomb. Hope is anchored to a moment in history when death itself was overcome. Hope does not predict outcomes. Hope proclaims that the One who governs outcomes is faithful. And because He is faithful, your suffering is not meaningless, your future is not abandoned, and your life is held in hands that have already conquered the grave.

This is why Christian hope can survive what optimism cannot. Optimism trembles when the road grows dark. Hope stands firm because the Light has already entered the darkness and cannot be overcome. Optimism depends on signs of improvement; hope depends on the God who promised, "I am with you always." Optimism feels threatened by sorrow; hope knows that sorrow has been touched by the Cross and therefore cannot swallow you. Optimism is emotional; hope is theological. Optimism falters when sickness persists; hope endures because it looks not at the body alone but at the God who will one day raise the body.

There is a moment in the Gospel of John when Jesus stands before the tomb of Lazarus. Martha, grief-stricken and weary, says to Him, "Lord, if You had been here, my brother would not have died." Beneath her words is the same quiet ache felt by every suffering heart: "If only God had acted sooner… if only the story had unfolded differently… if only this pain had been spared." Jesus does not rebuke her sorrow. He does not shame her questions. He does not demand optimism. Instead, He gives her the very thing that suffering needs in order to breathe again: hope. And not hope in better circumstances, but hope in Himself. "I am the resurrection and the life," He says. "Whoever believes in Me, though he die, yet shall he live" (John 11:25–26). This is not comfort based on outcomes. It is comfort based on identity. Jesus does not say, "Your brother will be fine." He says, "I am the Resurrection." Which is to say: no matter how dark this moment is, no matter how final death appears, no matter how deep your grief feels, I am Lord over even this.

Christian hope begins there—with the One who stands before every tomb and every diagnosis and every valley of fear and proclaims a truth stronger than everything you are facing: death does not have the final word. Suffering does not define your story. Fear does not control your destiny. The God who raised Jesus from the dead is the God who holds your life now. Hope is not wishful thinking. Hope is not "things will get better soon." Hope is "Christ is risen, and therefore I am not alone in this, not now, not ever."

St. Paul speaks with almost startling boldness when he writes, "If Christ has not been raised, then our preaching is in vain and your faith is in vain" (1 Corinthians 15:14). Paul does not anchor hope in psychological resilience or positive outcomes. He anchors it entirely in the Resurrection. For Paul, the Resurrection is not an inspiring symbol; it is the very fabric of Christian existence. Without it, suffering suffocates. Without it, death wins. Without it, the world is locked in despair. But with it—everything changes. With it, suffering is no longer the end of the story. With it, death is not a destination but a doorway. With it, hope becomes something stronger than fear, stronger than illness, stronger even than the grief that sickness creates.

This is why Christian hope can accompany you into the hardest rooms of your life. It can sit beside you in the clinic while you wait for your name to be called. It can steady your breathing when the doctor enters with results. It can hold your heart when you see numbers or scans that make your stomach tighten. It can remain when you wake at night and fear the future. Not because hope denies your suffering—it does not—but because hope knows that suffering is not the whole truth. Hope looks at the deepest wound and says, "Even here, Christ is Lord." Hope looks at the fragility of the body and says, "This weakness is not the measure of my life." Hope looks at the uncertainty of tomorrow and says, "My future is held by a God who has defeated death."

The difference between optimism and hope becomes clearest when you face moments that optimism cannot survive. Optimism breaks when you hear news that doesn't match your expectations. Optimism trembles when the road gets longer. Optimism feels betrayed when healing is delayed. But hope—true hope—remains. Hope stays not because it is strong but because its foundation is strong. Hope remains because Christ remains. Hope endures because the love of God endures. Hope survives because the tomb is empty.

When you feel overwhelmed, when the illness drags on, when fatigue and fear creep into your days, you may wonder whether you still have hope at all. The feelings of hope may fade. The emotional brightness may dim. But hope itself does not. Because hope is not a feeling. Hope is a Person. And that Person does not abandon His children. Christian hope is not the belief that things will turn out the way you desire. It is the unshakable trust that God will be with you no matter how they turn out. The difference is everything.

There is a moment in every believer's life when this truth becomes more than theology. It becomes breath. It becomes the steadying force that carries you through hours when you cannot steady yourself. It becomes the quiet conviction that even if the waves rise higher than you imagined, Christ is in the boat with you. This does not remove the storm, but it transforms what the storm can do. Illness may weaken your body, but it cannot sever you from the One who holds you. Pain may cloud your thoughts, but it cannot dim the truth of the Resurrection. Fear may whisper loudly in the night, but it cannot speak a word that overturns God's promise. The most fragile moment of your life is still held in the hands of the One who conquered death.

Hope, once understood in this way, does something profound within the heart. It lifts your eyes—not by denying your suffering, but by planting your suffering inside a larger story, a story where Christ has already gone ahead of you. You begin to see that your life is not suspended over a void, nor is it left to the cold calculations of chance. Your life rests on a foundation that does not crumble when the ground shifts beneath your feet. The Resurrection reshapes the very landscape of fear. Because if Christ is risen, then the darkest possibilities you imagine are not the end of your story. Even death, which once appeared as the final horizon, has been turned into a doorway through which you pass into the embrace of God. The Resurrection does not promise that your path will be free of suffering. It promises that suffering cannot imprison you.

Hope allows you to face illness without pretending. It gives you the honesty to say, "This is hard," while also saying, "This is not the whole truth." It frees you from needing to manufacture positivity. You do not need to smile when you are scared. You do not need to talk as though everything will unfold according to your desires. Hope does not require pretending. Hope requires trust. And trust does not mean understanding; it means leaning. Leaning on a God who has shown, in the most decisive way possible, that He will never abandon you. When Christ rose from the dead, He did not simply prove that life is stronger than death. He proved that love is stronger than fear. He proved that nothing—not illness, not disappointment, not the worst news a doctor can speak—can separate you from the love of God that is in Christ Jesus.

St. Paul learned this not from a comfortable life, but from a life marked by suffering. His body bore scars, his soul endured anxiety, his days were filled with pressures few of us can imagine. And yet he wrote with a clarity born from encounter: "We are afflicted in every way, but not crushed; perplexed, but not driven to despair... always carrying in the body the death of Jesus, so that the life of Jesus may also be manifested in us" (2 Corinthians 4:8–10). Paul's hope was not rooted in escape from suffering but in Christ's presence within it. He understood that hope is not the denial of reality; it is the deeper reality, the one that does not tremble when circumstances shift.

This is the kind of hope you are invited into now. A hope that understands your tears. A hope that does not scold your fears. A hope that does not collapse when treatment is difficult or when results are uncertain. A hope that meets you in the doctor's office, in the waiting room, in the long hours at home when you are too tired to stand. A hope that enters your weakness and sits with you quietly. A hope that can hold questions without offering clichés. A hope that looks at Jesus and says, "Because You live, I can face what is in front of me."

There will still be days when hope feels thin. That does not mean it is gone. The feeling of hope rises and falls; the reality of hope does not. The root of hope is not in your chest—it is in Christ's empty tomb. And the tomb does not refill itself when you feel discouraged. It remains empty, whether your heart feels strong or fragile. This is why hope can outlast every wave of fear. Its foundation is immovable. Its substance is Christ Himself.

And slowly, as you walk forward with this truth beneath your feet, your soul begins to breathe again. Not with naïve positivity, but with a steadiness that grows from knowing you are upheld by something stronger than circumstance. You may still pray for healing; of course you will. You may still pray for strength, for relief, for good news. And God hears every one of those prayers with tenderness. But beneath all these prayers, beneath all the longing and the fear and the exhaustion, something deeper has taken root: the assurance that no matter what tomorrow holds, God will meet you there. You will not walk into any day alone.

Hope is not the refusal to suffer. It is the refusal to believe that suffering has the final word. Hope is the conviction that Christ is Lord not only over your joys but over your sorrows. Hope is the courage to believe that even the hardest chapters of your life can become places where God draws nearer. Hope is the quiet strength that says, "I do not know what comes next, but I know who comes with me."

This hope, born of the Resurrection, does not collapse beneath the weight of illness. It does not fade when the future feels uncertain. It does not disappear when your emotions weaken. It stands because Christ stands. It lives because Christ lives. It endures because Christ's victory is not undone by the trials His children face.

And so, as you continue along this path, let this truth settle into the deepest place of your heart: optimism may falter, but hope endures. Optimism may crumble, but hope holds. Optimism may fear disappointment, but hope fears nothing—not because the future is predictable, but because the One who holds the future is faithful. The final word over your life is not cancer. The final word is Christ. And that word is life.

Twelve

What Your Suffering Does Not Take Away

Illness has a way of touching places in the heart we never realised were vulnerable. It can begin with something as simple as fatigue, a weakness you cannot quite push through, or the quiet disappointment of discovering you cannot do today what you did easily a year ago. As the body changes, as symptoms rise and fall, as the mirror shows someone who looks more tired than you remember, there can emerge an unspoken fear: "Am I becoming less myself?" No doctor mentions this question, but it hangs over the bed, over the long hours of waiting, over the hum of machines in treatment rooms. It rises from the very centre of the human experience of suffering. When health is shaken, identity feels shaken with it. When strength fades, a person can begin to wonder whether their worth is fading too. And yet the truth of the Gospel speaks directly, tenderly, and unequivocally into this fear: your suffering cannot take away who you are. It cannot diminish your dignity. It cannot touch the image of God in you. It cannot reach into the place where God has named you His own.

If anything in this chapter matters, it is this: you are loved the same on your weak days as on your strong ones. Love does not measure you by your stamina. God does not value you according to your productivity or energy or independence. Love is not a reward for performance; it is the truth of your existence. Before you ever accomplished anything, before you ever proved anything, before a single achievement or milestone or contribution marked your life, God spoke a word over you: "You are Mine." That word has never wavered. The circumstances of your body may shift, but God's affection does not tremble in the slightest. Illness may alter your schedule, your abilities, your routines, your strength, but it cannot alter God's heart toward you. Cancer can touch many things, but it cannot touch the love of God.

There is a reason Scripture speaks of God's love in covenant terms rather than emotional ones. Emotions rise and fall. Circumstances change overnight. Health follows seasons that sometimes cannot be predicted. Yet God binds Himself to His people not with fleeting sentiment but with a promise: "I have called you by name; you are Mine" (Isaiah 43:1). Nothing in your body, nothing in your diagnosis, nothing in your weakness can change the reality of being known and loved by God. When you feel depleted, God does not see less of you; He sees more, because the heart becomes transparent in suffering. When you feel like your life has narrowed, God sees you walking a path He Himself walked in Christ. When you feel like you are becoming a burden, God reminds you that the whole story of salvation is built on the truth that human beings were never meant to carry life alone.

The imago Dei — the image of God — is not held in your muscles, your energy, or your resilience. It is not diminished by fatigue or reshaped by illness. The image of God is held in the soul, and nothing on earth can lay a hand on it. This truth is the bedrock beneath your feet when so much else feels unsteady. You may feel physically weakened, emotionally overwhelmed, or spiritually drained, but the deepest part of you remains untouched and radiant with the dignity God Himself bestowed. This dignity is not a fragile thing. It is not delicate. It is not something you can lose in a hospital room or surrender in the face of medical appointments. It is as enduring as the God whose image you bear.

There is a quiet lie that suffering tries to smuggle into the heart, a lie that whispers that weakness somehow makes a person less valuable. This lie thrives on comparison — comparing your present self to your past self, comparing your abilities now to the abilities you once took for granted. The world often prizes strength, independence, productivity, and outward accomplishment, and when illness strikes, it can feel as though these worldly measures of worth slip through your fingers. But the Gospel overturns those measures entirely. In God's eyes, strength has never been the currency of worth. Holiness has never been about living without limits. Value has never been determined by what you can do. From the beginning, dignity has been rooted not in what you accomplish but in who created you, loved you, and claimed you.

Suffering does not peel away your identity; it reveals the truth of it. When life is comfortable, a hundred distractions crowd the heart. You can busy yourself with plans, projects, goals, to-do lists, responsibilities, and expectations. These things are not bad, but they can become layers that mask who you are beneath them. When illness enters the story, those layers begin to fall away. You see yourself more clearly — not because you have lost something essential, but because the noise around the essential has quieted. You learn that your humanity is not tied to your efficiency, that your worth is not tied to your independence, that your identity is not tied to your physical strength. You discover that the soul — which is the truest part of you — often shines most clearly when the body is weakest.

There is a reason that the saints, in their times of trial, often became more visibly themselves, not less. Job stood in ashes yet spoke with a clarity of faith unseen in his days of prosperity. Mary stood beneath the Cross in a radiant posture of love, though every earthly sign pointed to loss. Christ Himself revealed the depths of divine compassion most clearly not in His miracles but in His suffering — in His silence before His accusers, in His endurance on the road to Calvary, in His willingness to be held by the Father when everything else was stripped away. Suffering did not diminish Him; it revealed Him. And though your suffering is different in kind and purpose, it carries a similar truth: when things fall away, what is most real in you has the chance to be seen.

Perhaps one of the most painful fears that arises during illness is the fear of becoming a burden. This fear is quiet, personal, and often hidden from others. It grows out of a noble heart — a heart that wants to protect the people it loves, a heart that wants to give more than it receives, a heart that once found joy in caring for others and now grieves needing to be cared for. Yet needing help does not make you a burden. It makes you human. Even Jesus, in His Passion, received help He did not "need" in His divine strength: Simon of Cyrene carried His Cross; Veronica wiped His face; the women of Jerusalem wept for Him. The Son of God allowed others to minister to Him because humility is not weakness — it is love. When you allow others to help you, you give them the gift of becoming Christ-like. You open the door for grace to pass between hearts. You show them what compassion is for, and you allow love to take a shape it could never have taken if you were never in need.

Love grows when dependence is acknowledged. Community deepens when vulnerability is shared. Families become more tender when they walk through suffering together. And your willingness to receive care becomes a silent witness to everyone around you that dignity does not disappear when life becomes fragile. On the contrary:

dignity takes on a new depth. It becomes luminous in a way it never could have been in seasons of ease.

Identity is not bestowed by health, and therefore illness cannot take it away. You are not defined by medical charts, by bloodwork, by scan results, by energy levels. You are not reduced to your diagnosis. You are not the sum of your limitations. You are God's beloved child — yesterday, today, and tomorrow — and nothing in creation, nothing in suffering, nothing in human frailty, nothing in the rise or fall of your strength can undo this truth. Your body may feel fragile, but your identity is not. Your days may feel uncertain, but your dignity is not. You are still who you have always been: created, chosen, loved, upheld.

Your suffering does not diminish your story. It deepens it. It becomes the place where God meets you more tenderly, more personally, more faithfully than you ever imagined He would. And as you walk this path, there is not a moment — not one breath, not one tear, not one fear — that He overlooks or abandons. You remain held in the love that called you into being.

Your worth does not tremble when your body trembles. Your dignity does not weaken when your muscles do. Your identity does not fade when fatigue sets in. There is a truth older than every ache, deeper than every diagnosis, stronger than every limitation: before you were ever sick, before you ever feared the future, before a single doctor spoke a difficult word, God looked upon you and saw His image. That image remains. That image shines. That image is not dimmed by anything your body endures. Suffering can shadow many things, but it cannot shadow the soul. The imago Dei was breathed into you at creation, sealed in you at baptism, strengthened in you every time grace touched your life. No illness can rewrite that story.

It is one thing to know this theologically and another to feel it when your strength runs thin. Some days you may look in the mirror and struggle to recognise the person staring back. Some days you may feel that you have lost parts of yourself — your energy, your independence, your familiar routines, your sense of certainty. Yet these things, precious as they are, were never the core of who you are. They were gifts, not identity. The core remains untouched. You are not less yourself because your body suffers. You are not less loved because you cannot do what you once did. You are not less worthy because you need help. Identity rooted in God cannot be diminished by anything that is not God.

If you ever fear you are "disappearing," remember this: suffering does not erase the person; it reveals the person. Think of gold being purified, not by comfort but by fire. The fire does not create the gold; it reveals what was already there. In your own suffering, something similar happens. The strength you never knew you had begins to appear. The humility you rarely needed before takes gentle root. The patience you never asked for but now practice daily becomes part of your witness. The compassion that others show you becomes a mirror reflecting how deeply you are loved. The love you show them, even in exhaustion, becomes a testimony more powerful than any words. Suffering uncovers who you are — not the part of you the world sees, but the part of you God sees. The depth. The resilience. The quiet courage. The long endurance that holds onto God even when all you can manage is a whisper.

People often think suffering diminishes a person. In truth, it strips away illusions. It reveals that the human person is not defined by strength but by love. Not by productivity but by relationship. Not by independence but by communion. When God created humanity, He said, "Let Us make man in Our image." That image was relational from the start — born of the eternal communion of Father, Son, and Spirit. Illness may remove the ability to do many things, but it cannot remove the capacity to love or to be loved. In fact, these capacities often grow stronger in times of weakness. You may find that family members hold you more tenderly, that friendships deepen, that conversations become more honest, that presence becomes more precious. You may discover that moments once taken for granted now carry a weight of grace you never expected. And through it all, your dignity is not eroded — it becomes more visible.

One of the quiet graces of illness is that it reveals how deeply others cherish you. People may express their love with words they never spoke before. They may show their love through actions that surprise you. They may sit at your bedside, speak gently to you, pray for you, or simply accompany you in silence. Do not dismiss these things. They are sacraments in their own way — outward signs of hidden grace. They reveal something God has always known about you: that you are worth loving, not because of what you can do, but because of who you are. Your existence is a gift to others even when you cannot "give" anything in return. Love does not ask for performance. Love delights in the beloved. When others care for you, they are not carrying a burden; they are carrying a treasure.

Sometimes you may feel the opposite — that the people around you carry too much, worry too much, spend too much time and energy helping you. You may wish you could do more, carry more, spare them more. These feelings are natural, and God sees them with compassion. Yet He also invites you to see care from another angle: letting others love you is not a failure. It is humility. It is trust. It is the way grace circulates through the Body of Christ. When you allow others to support you, you teach them how to be Christ-like. When you let them pray for you, you open a channel for grace to flow that would otherwise remain closed. When you accept help, you draw others into the mystery of love that Christ revealed when He allowed Simon of Cyrene to lift His Cross.

Your presence — even in weakness — is a blessing. Your life speaks a truth more powerful than any sermon: that the dignity of the human person is not measured by worldly standards. Not by productivity. Not by physical capacity. Not by independence. Dignity is rooted in God alone. And because God does not change, your dignity does not either.

If you ever wonder who you are now, the answer is the same as it was before illness entered your life. You are God's child. You are God's beloved. You are the one for whom Christ died and rose. You are the one whose tears are counted, whose fears are heard, whose suffering is held with infinite tenderness. You are the one who bears God's image — an image cancer cannot touch. You are the one whose life has meaning even in pain, whose existence carries weight even in silence, whose story has purpose even in weakness. The world may see fragility. God sees beauty. The world may see limitation. God sees the opening of the heart. The world may see decline. God sees the shaping of a soul into the likeness of His Son.

The illness you face can change many things — your plans, your strength, your pace, your days — but it cannot change the truth of who you are. It cannot diminish your value. It cannot erase your identity. It cannot touch the image of God that shines in the very centre of your being. You remain, now and always, God's beloved child. Your suffering does not diminish your story; it deepens it. Your weakness does not make you less yourself; it reveals the person God has been loving all along. And in that love, which illness cannot reach, your dignity stands secure forever.

Thirteen

God's Power in Weakness

Weakness is one of the few experiences in life you never truly prepare for. It comes slowly at first, almost quietly, until one day you realise that ordinary tasks have become heavier, that decisions take more energy than before, that even waking in the morning feels like lifting something far beyond your strength. Illness has a way of humbling the body and the heart together. It exposes limits you never had to acknowledge, invites dependence you never wished to need, and reveals how fragile even the strongest person can feel when the weight of suffering settles in the bones. Many people interpret this weakness as a spiritual failure, a loss of dignity, a sign that God must surely be disappointed or distant. Yet Scripture insists on the opposite. Weakness is not the place where God withdraws. It is the place where God draws near. It is not the end of spiritual life but the beginning of a deeper one. Weakness is not a disqualification; it is the very soil in which grace chooses to grow.

No biblical figure teaches this more clearly than St. Paul. Paul was not a man unfamiliar with suffering. He endured imprisonment, beatings, shipwrecks, rejection, hunger, sleepless nights, and fear. But there was something else—something more personal—that Scripture simply calls a "thorn in the flesh" (2 Corinthians 12:7). We are not told exactly what it was, and perhaps that is God's mercy, because it allows every suffering believer to recognise themselves in Paul. It might have been physical pain, or chronic illness, or weakness that embarrassed him, or a disability he could not overcome, or even a spiritual heaviness that pulled on him throughout his ministry. Whatever it was, Paul prayed the way any suffering soul would pray. He did not ask once. He did not ask twice. He begged God three times to take it away. Scripture uses the Greek term *parekalesa*, meaning he pleaded — he implored — not calmly, but with raw intensity, the way a person in deep pain cries out for relief.

And here is the comfort: Paul did not pretend to be strong. He did not try to endure silently. He did not shame himself for wanting healing. He did exactly what the suffering believer does — he went to God with an honest heart and said, "Lord, this is too much for me. Please remove it." There is no rebuke in that request. It is not lack of faith. It is faith expressed in its most vulnerable form: the child asking the Father for mercy.

Yet God's answer was not what Paul expected. Scripture says: *"But He said to me, 'My grace is sufficient for you, for My power is made perfect in weakness'"* (2 Cor 12:9). These are among the most mysterious and consoling words in the entire Bible. God did not say, "Your suffering is small; stop complaining." He did not say, "You should be stronger." He did not say, "Try harder, Paul." He did not even say, "One day I will remove it." He said something infinitely more profound: My grace is enough. Not in the future, not when you feel better, not when the illness lifts — now. My grace does not supplement your strength. My grace fills your lack of it. And then the most astonishing line: My power is made perfect — not in your gifts, not in your resilience, not in your endurance, not in your achievements — but in your weakness.

This is how radically different God's vision of your life is from the world's. The world treasures strength, independence, self-assurance, and bodily capability. God treasures surrender, humility, dependence, and trust. Strength impresses people; weakness invites God. The world says, "You are valuable when you are strong." God says, "You are lovable when you are Mine — and weakness only draws Me closer." Paul's experience becomes a mirror in which every suffering soul can see themselves. When your body weakens, when fatigue overcomes you, when you feel embarrassed by what you cannot do anymore, when you fear that you are becoming a burden — the thorn in Paul's flesh whispers to you across centuries: You are exactly where God's power loves to rest.

And this is not an isolated moment in Scripture. It is the pattern of salvation history. God chooses Moses, who cannot speak clearly, to confront Pharaoh. The book of Exodus tells us that Moses protested, "*I am slow of speech and of tongue*" (Ex 4:10), but God's reply was not, "I will fix you," but "I will be with you." God chooses Gideon, who calls himself the least of his household and the weakest of his tribe, to defeat an army far larger than his own. God chooses David, the youngest shepherd boy, overlooked even by his own father, to be king. God chooses Mary, a poor young woman from Nazareth, to bear His Son. God chooses fishermen — not scholars, not priests, not the powerful — to become apostles. God chooses the Cross — the ultimate symbol of weakness, helplessness, and humiliation — as the place of triumph over sin and death. Over and over again, God shows that His work does not flow through human strength. It flows through human surrender.

A person suffering from cancer understands this pattern in a way few others can. Illness dismantles every illusion that we control our own lives. It humbles us, not because we have done anything wrong, but because our bodies are fragile and the world is broken. Yet in that fragility, something sacred opens. When your strength fades, pride releases its grip. When pride releases its grip, the soul becomes porous. And when the soul becomes porous, grace seeps into places that strength once sealed shut. This is why the saints speak so tenderly of weakness, not because they romanticised suffering, but because they discovered in their own trials what Paul discovered in his: that weakness is not the absence of God — it is the landing place of God.

There is a moment in the Gospels that reveals this with startling clarity. In the Garden of Gethsemane, Jesus does not pray from a position of strength. He prays from exhaustion. Luke tells us His sweat became like drops of blood. He fell to the ground. He trembled under the weight of what was coming. He prayed, *"Father, if You are willing, remove this cup from Me; nevertheless, not My will, but Yours be done"* (Lk 22:42). The eternal Son of God did not hide His weakness. He embraced it. And what happened then? Scripture says, *"An angel from heaven strengthened Him"* (Lk 22:43). Strength came — not before the weakness, but in the weakness.

What happened to Jesus in Gethsemane happens to every believer who enters the night carrying fear, pain, and weariness. God does not swoop in to remove every sorrow immediately; He comes to be with you in the sorrow. He does not replace weakness with human strength; He fills weakness with divine strength. He does not take away the cup; He shares it. And once He shares it, you are no longer drinking alone.

This is why your weakness does not diminish your spiritual life. It deepens it. When you cannot hold yourself up, God holds you. When you cannot pray, Christ prays within you. When you cannot find courage, the Holy Spirit breathes it quietly into your heart. When you cannot imagine the future, God stands in the future and waits for you there. Where others see fragility, God sees an opening. Where others see decline, God sees the chance for a new depth of intimacy. Where others see loss of strength, God sees a sanctuary forming — a place where His presence can rest more deeply than ever before.

Paul eventually reached a point where he no longer begged God to remove the thorn. Not because he grew numb, not because he stopped desiring healing, but because he realised that Christ had entered his weakness so fully that the weakness had become holy ground. This is why he could say, *"I will boast all the more gladly of my weaknesses, so that the power of Christ may rest upon me"* (2 Cor 12:9). The Greek word Paul uses for "rest" — *episkenoō* — means to pitch a tent, to dwell, to spread one's covering over. Weakness becomes the place Christ makes His home.

And if Paul's weakness became a dwelling place for Christ, then so can yours.

Weakness, then, is not an empty space waiting to be filled with your own effort; it is a sacred space waiting to be filled with God's presence. It is the place where heaven bends low, where grace descends quietly, where Christ chooses to dwell not because you are strong enough to host Him, but because you are weak enough to need Him. Your weakness is not the crack in your life; it is the place where divine light slips through.

Sometimes this truth is easier to accept with the mind than with the heart. Illness makes you feel exposed. The simplest tasks can feel impossible. You may find yourself needing help for things you once did without thinking. You might feel embarrassed at what your body can no longer do. You might fear that others see you differently now, or that you are somehow "less" because your strength has faded. The human heart often equates ability with dignity, independence with worth. But this is not the way God sees you. This is not the way love sees you. You do not lose dignity when you lose strength. You do not lose worth when you need help. You are not becoming less in God's eyes — you are becoming more transparent to His grace.

St. Thomas Aquinas wrote that God allows weakness in His children not to diminish them but to "draw them more perfectly into His love." Weakness makes room for God. The stronger a person feels, the easier it is to forget how dependent we truly are. But when illness strips away the illusion of self-sufficiency, you stand before God the way you were always meant to stand: as one who needs Him, one who relies on Him, one who is held together moment by moment by His mercy. There is no shame in this. This is the truth of the human condition. Even the healthiest person in the world is fragile compared to the One who spoke galaxies into existence.

And if weakness opens the door for grace, it also opens the door for compassion — both given and received. When you are weak, your family sees your courage more clearly. Your friends see your perseverance more honestly. Love becomes deeper because it becomes shared. You are teaching others — without even realising it — how to love generously, how to serve without expectation, how to honour the dignity of another person's vulnerability. Weakness is not simply something you endure; it becomes something your life proclaims: *Love is stronger than loss. Grace is stronger than decay. Christ is stronger than the fear that haunts the sickroom.*

This is one of the mysteries of suffering. It reveals the truth of the soul. Strength hides things; weakness reveals them. When a person suffers with patience, others see courage. When a person suffers with faith, others see trust. When a person suffers with love, others see Christ. Cancer cannot dim that light. If anything, it makes it shine more clearly against the backdrop of pain. God's power is not visible when everything is easy; it becomes visible when everything is hard. You are living a mystery that angels marvel to see — because in your weakness, the glory of God is being made known.

But perhaps the most consoling truth is this: weakness unites you to Christ in a way nothing else can. We often think the closest moments to Jesus are those filled with joy, peace, or spiritual strength. Yet Scripture points again and again to a different kind of closeness — the closeness of shared suffering. Isaiah calls Him "a man of sorrows, acquainted with grief" (Isaiah 53:3). The Letter to the Hebrews says He was made like us "in every respect" so He might become a merciful High Priest who understands our weakness (Hebrews 4:15). Christ knows the weight of frailty from the inside. He knows exhaustion. He knows pain. He knows the trembling of the human heart. He knows what it means to feel alone, to feel pressed beyond strength, to feel the body fail beneath Him. On the Cross, He entered weakness more fully than any human being ever has — not so that we would never experience it, but so that when we do, we find Him already there.

Your weakness is not a place Christ avoids. It is the place where He meets you most intimately. Every sigh, every tear, every moment of fatigue is known by Him with tenderness. He does not rush you through your weakness or demand that you rise above it. He accompanies you inside it. Suffering is not the sign that God is far; it is the place where God reveals how close He has always been.

This nearness of Christ transforms the meaning of weakness. It does not make the experience easy, but it fills it with purpose. You are sharing in Christ's own suffering, and Scripture promises that those who share His sufferings will also share His glory (Romans 8:17). Weakness becomes a participation in the love that redeemed the world. The very place you feel most helpless is the place where God is doing His deepest work — shaping your soul, sanctifying your heart, and drawing you into a love that is stronger than death.

Paul eventually reached the point where he could say words that at first seem impossible: *"I will boast all the more gladly of my weaknesses, so that the power of Christ may rest upon me."* He was not glorifying pain; he was glorifying the Presence who filled the pain. He discovered that Christ rested most deeply not in the parts of him that were strong, but in the parts that were weak. That is where grace builds its home.

And this is true for you as well. You may not feel powerful. You may not feel strong. You may not feel capable of great spiritual acts. But Christ is not asking for power from you. He is offering His power to you. He is not asking for your strength. He is offering His strength. Your weakness is not where God stops working — it is where God begins. When the world sees a failing body, heaven sees a soul being readied for glory. When the world sees decline, God sees sanctification. When the world sees fragility, God sees a child resting in the arms of the Father.

Weakness, then, becomes a hidden sanctuary. It becomes a place where the noise of achievement, success, and self-reliance finally quiets, and the whisper of God's love can be heard more clearly. It becomes a place where trust is born — real trust, not the kind we offer when life is smooth, but the trust that emerges only when everything familiar gives way and all that remains is the God who holds your life in His hands.

And here, in this place of weakness, you discover the deepest truth of all:

You are not defined by what you can do. You are defined by the One who loves you.

Your strength may fade, but His does not. Your body may weaken, but His grace does not. Your abilities may change, but His affection does not.

You are safe in His hands — not when you are strong, but precisely when you are weak.

God's power is not waiting for your recovery; it is resting upon you now.

Fourteen

Nothing Is Wasted

There is a quiet question that rises in nearly every suffering heart, a question so tender and so raw that most people hesitate to speak it aloud. It is not a theological puzzle or a philosophical inquiry. It is the question of a soul searching for meaning while carrying a weight it never asked to bear. It whispers through hospital rooms, waiting rooms, dark nights, and long days that seem to blend into one another: *Does any of this matter? Is anything happening here, or is my pain simply falling into the silence? Does God see? Does God use this? Or is all of this—every tear, every fear, every hour of exhaustion—simply wasted?* This longing for meaning is not a flaw in the human heart; it is a sign of how deeply we are made for purpose. We want to believe that our suffering is not just endured but somehow transformed, somehow noticed, somehow taken up into a story larger than our own.

And Scripture, in its unflinching honesty, answers this longing not with vague reassurances but with a promise so intimate and so tender that it almost feels impossible to be true. The psalmist dares to say, *"You have kept count of my tossing's; put my tears in Your bottle"* (Psalm

56:8). Not one sigh is lost. Not one tear is ignored. Not one moment of restlessness or fear escapes the attention of the God who numbers the hairs of your head. In the ancient world, keeping someone's tears in a bottle was a sign of treasured remembrance—an expression of love so deep that one preserved the evidence of another's sorrow as something precious, something worth holding onto. When Scripture says that God gathers your tears, it is telling you that nothing in your suffering is unnoticed, nothing is discarded, nothing is too small to matter to the One who loves you more than you love yourself.

God is not a distant observer of your suffering. He is the Keeper of your tears. This means your pain is not anonymous. It is not swallowed by the cold mechanics of the universe. It is known by name. It is held in the hands that shaped the stars. Long before you asked the question, "Is this wasted?" God had already answered: *Nothing you endure is lost. Nothing you give in love is forgotten. Nothing you suffer is without meaning in My eyes.*

But the human heart struggles to believe this, because suffering feels so empty. Pain feels barren. Illness feels like a long season of subtraction—less energy, less independence, less clarity, less control. It is hard to imagine that something fruitful could grow in soil that feels so barren. And yet the pattern of God's work has always been to bring something living out of places that look dead. The Scriptures are filled with barren women who become mothers, deserts that bloom with streams of water, exiles who return home with songs, crosses that become thrones of victory. God has never needed strong soil to grow His miracles. He only needs surrendered soil. And suffering, for all its heaviness, often becomes the most surrendered soil of all.

When Jesus fed the five thousand, John tells us that after everyone had eaten and was satisfied, Jesus turned to His disciples and said, *"Gather up the fragments, that nothing may be lost"* (John 6:12). Those words—simple, almost practical—are charged with a spiritual truth.

Christ wastes nothing. If He commands the gathering of leftover pieces of bread, how much more does He gather the fragments of your suffering? If He does not allow crumbs to fall unnoticed, how much more carefully does He guard the tears of His beloved? Nothing in your life is insignificant to Him. Nothing. The sleepless night. The quiet courage of showing up to another appointment. The pain you endure without complaint. The fear you hand to Him in a whisper. The patience you offer to those who care for you. The hope you cling to even when it flickers. These are not small things to God. These are offerings. These are seeds. These are fragments that Christ gathers so that nothing—absolutely nothing—may be lost.

But maybe you wonder, *What could God possibly do with this? How can my pain bring about anything good? How can cancer, of all things, become part of God's work?* It is the same question Paul must have asked when he wrote from prison, bearing wounds and hardships that would have broken almost anyone else: *"I rejoice in my sufferings for your sake, and in my flesh I complete what is lacking in Christ's afflictions"* (Colossians 1:24). Paul was not claiming to add to the infinite value of Christ's sacrifice. He was saying that Christ allows His followers to share in His suffering in such a way that their pain becomes a channel of His grace. Christ does not suffer *instead* of us or *apart* from us; He suffers *within* us, and He transforms that suffering into love that radiates outward. This is the mystery of redemptive suffering—not that we earn salvation through pain, but that our pain, united to Christ's, becomes part of His redeeming love poured into the world.

Nothing is more humbling or more dignifying than this truth. Your suffering is not pointless. It is not meaningless. It is not wasted. Christ has taken it into His own suffering, the suffering through which He saved the world. When you offer even a small part of your pain to Him—"Jesus, I give You this hour," "Lord, use this for someone who needs grace today," "Christ, take this fear and turn it into mercy for someone else"—He receives it as something infinitely precious, and He weaves it into His work of healing, sanctifying, strengthening, and saving souls. You may not see the fruit in this life, but heaven will reveal that the smallest offering made in suffering became light for someone living in darkness, strength for someone who had none, peace for someone crying out for help. Nothing is wasted because Christ wastes nothing.

St. Augustine once wrote, "God does not permit evil except to draw from it a greater good." He was not minimizing evil; he was testifying to God's power. If God could draw the redemption of the world from the torture and death of His Son, then He can draw good from the suffering that overwhelms you now. The Cross did not look meaningful on Good Friday. It looked like defeat, injustice, horror, and abandonment. But in that moment, hidden from human eyes, God was doing His greatest work. The world saw only loss. Heaven saw victory taking root. In the same way, your suffering may look barren to you now, but God is at work in hidden ways—work that may only become visible in the light of eternity.

And there is something else, something just as beautiful: suffering reveals the soul in a way comfort never can. People who suffer with faith become a kind of living homily. Their quiet endurance speaks louder than sermons. Their small acts of trust become like candles in the darkness. Their perseverance gives courage to others. Their tears soften hard hearts. Their humility and dependence call forth compassion in those around them. Even their silent witness—simply holding onto God in the midst of pain—becomes a testimony that touches lives without them ever realising it. This is why Jesus said, "Let your light shine before others" (Matthew 5:16). Sometimes that light shines through joy. But often, the brightest light shines through suffering.

And yet the fear remains: *What if none of this matters? What if my* strength is fading and I have nothing left to give? What if everything I endure is simply falling into the void? It is here that the promise of Romans 8:28 becomes more than a verse we quote—it becomes a lifeline. *"We know that in everything God works for good for those who love Him."* Not in some things. Not in the pleasant things. Not in the moments that feel spiritual. In **everything**. Even illness. Even sorrow. Even exhaustion. Even weakness. God does not cause your suffering, but He enters it, and once He enters it, He uses it—not for punishment, not for shame, not for despair, but for a good so deep and so hidden that only eternity will reveal its full glory.

It may feel, at times, as though your suffering is happening in isolation, as though the world goes on while you sit inside a story that no one else can quite understand. Yet heaven is far closer, far more attentive, far more involved than your senses can perceive. The God who keeps your tears in His bottle is not tallying them like an accountant; He is treasuring them like a Father. Every moment of endurance, every quiet offering, every trembling prayer becomes a thread God weaves into a tapestry you cannot yet see. What feels to you like weakness is often, in His hands, a hidden act of love with consequences you may never know on this side of eternity. The saints tell us that grace is never confined to the one who suffers; it spreads outward, touching lives in ways unseen. A sickbed can become a pulpit. A whispered prayer can become a shield for someone far away. A single act of patient endurance can open a flood of grace for a soul on the brink of despair. If this seems impossible, remember: the whole Christian mystery is built on something that looked wasted—Christ's suffering—and yet became the source of life for the world.

There is a quiet power in suffering endured with love, even when the love feels small or fragile. Sometimes all you can offer God is your breath, your presence, your willingness to endure one more hour with Him. That is enough. God does not measure the value of your offering by its size but by its sincerity. The widow's mite was worth more to Him than the large gifts of the wealthy because it came from the heart. Your suffering, offered in faith, is the widow's mite of your life—not because it is small, but because it is everything you have in this moment. And God receives it with the same tenderness with which Jesus received that widow's coin. He sees the cost. He sees the love beneath the struggle. He sees the trust beneath the fear. Nothing is wasted that is given to God, no matter how incomplete or broken it feels to you.

Christ Himself reveals this truth more clearly than any argument ever could. When He gathered His apostles at the Last Supper, He took bread—something ordinary, breakable, perishable—and He blessed it, broke it, and said, "This is My Body." He transformed something fragile into a vessel of eternal grace. Then, on the Cross, He allowed His own Body to be broken in the ultimate act of love. Brokenness did not diminish His gift; it revealed it. His suffering was not wasted. It became the place where divine love reached its fullest expression. If God could take the broken Body of His Son and make it the source of salvation, then He can take the broken places in your life and make them sources of grace as well. Not by erasing your pain, but by filling it with His presence. Not by eliminating your suffering, but by entering it so fully that it becomes united to His own.

And because Christ has entered your suffering, your suffering now has a depth it never had before. It participates in His. This is what Paul meant when he said he "rejoiced" in his sufferings—not because pain is joyful, but because love is. He saw his trials as a way of being drawn into deeper union with Christ, of allowing Christ's love to flow through him, even—and especially—when he was weak. Your suffering does the same. It becomes a place where Christ can love through you. It becomes a quiet offering that strengthens others, even if you never see how. It becomes an act of intercession more powerful than words.

It becomes a light that God uses to push back the darkness in someone else's life.

This is why nothing is wasted. Suffering, when united to Christ, becomes seed planted in the soil of eternity. You may never see the fruit in this life, but God sees it already. He knows exactly what your suffering is accomplishing, even if you do not. He knows whom it is helping, whom it is strengthening, whom it is healing. He knows the graces He is pouring out through your endurance, even when endurance feels like simply surviving the next minute. What you see as emptiness may be, in His hands, a chalice overflowing.

And still, there are days when meaning feels far away, when you do not sense anything holy or purposeful in what you are enduring. There are days when the pain is simply pain, when exhaustion is simply exhaustion, when tears come not as offerings but as reflexes of a heart stretched thin. On those days, you may feel as though all of this talk of purpose and redemption is meant for someone stronger than you, someone holier, someone who knows how to suffer well. But that is not the truth. The truth is that God does His greatest work not when you feel strong, but when you feel too weak to pretend. The moments you think are spiritually barren are often the moments heaven pays the closest attention. God is not waiting for you to produce something beautiful out of your suffering; He is producing something beautiful out of it Himself.

There is a reason the psalmist says that God "remembers" our frame and "knows that we are dust" (Psalm 103:14). He knows your limits better than you do. He knows when fatigue is too heavy to lift your thoughts. He knows when pain disrupts your focus. He knows when fears crowd the mind. And He does not measure you by what you achieve in these moments. He measures you by the truth that you are His. Your identity does not come from what you accomplish but from who holds you. A child does not stop being a child when they are sick or weak. They often become more deeply cherished. So it is with you. Your suffering does not make you less in God's eyes; it draws you more tenderly into His embrace.

This is why even the smallest act of faith during suffering carries such immense weight. A whispered "Jesus, help me." A hand lifted silently in prayer. A moment when you choose not to give up. A breath offered to God when breath itself is a battle. These are not minor gestures. They are the very substance of love. They are your heart reaching—however faintly—toward the One who is already holding you. If you could see how heaven responds to these offerings, how the angels stand in awe at the courage it takes simply to trust when trust feels impossible, you would never again doubt that your suffering is accomplishing something eternal.

Even the tears you shed in secret have a purpose. Scripture does not say God counts your victories; it says He counts your tears. Tears are the language of the soul when words fail. They are prayers without syllables, sacrifices without form, confessions without shape. In God's eyes, they are precious. They water the soil where grace takes root. They carry the weight of love, longing, and surrender more honestly than any eloquent prayer. If God gathers each tear, then there is nothing in your suffering too small to be treasured.

You are walking a path that Christ Himself walked. He knows what it means to be weary. He knows what it means to cry out in the night. He knows what it means to feel isolated, misunderstood, and overwhelmed. And because He knows, He transforms. When you unite your suffering to His—consciously or simply by enduring it with faith—He takes your offering and breathes His Spirit through it. What you give Him in weakness, He returns in glory. What you surrender in pain, He turns into mercy. What you endure silently, He uses to speak hope into places you may never see.

So when the question rises again—*Is any of this doing anything? Is this all meaningless?*—let your heart answer with the truth God has spoken from the beginning: nothing surrendered to Him is lost. Nothing borne with Him is wasted. Nothing endured in love is forgotten. Your suffering is not a pause in your life's story; it is a chapter God is writing with infinite tenderness, a chapter whose meaning may be hidden now but will one day be luminous. Every moment you endure is carried into eternity, where it will shine with a brightness that can only be understood on the other side of this life.

There will come a day when you stand in the presence of God and see what He saw in every hour of your suffering. There will come a day when you understand how your quiet endurance strengthened someone else, how your faith in darkness gave light to another soul, how your tears watered seeds of grace that blossomed far beyond your sight. There will come a day when everything hidden is revealed and everything painful is healed. And on that day, you will know with absolute certainty that nothing—nothing—was wasted.

Until then, you walk with a God who gathers your fragments, who treasures your tears, who transforms your offerings, and who wastes nothing of the life He loves.

Fifteen

Love Rising From Hope

Hope does something subtle within the soul, something that cannot be reduced to a feeling or measured by outward signs. It changes the way the heart listens. After walking through the truths of Part III, you begin to sense—quietly, almost imperceptibly—that your suffering is no longer an isolated experience suspended in darkness. Hope allows you to see that your story is still unfolding, that God remains at work even when you cannot see the movement of His hand. It is not the loud hope of triumph or quick solutions. It is not the shallow hope that denies the reality of pain. It is the hope born from discovering that God has been with you in every weakness, in every tear, in every moment when you feared the road had become too hard to walk. Hope is the steadying presence that tells the heart, "You are not abandoned. You have never been abandoned. Even this—especially this—is known by God."

As this truth settles, your suffering takes on a different texture. The questions that once felt sharp begin to soften. You no longer demand answers with the urgency that once consumed you. Something in you begins to trust that God is holding what you cannot hold. You may not understand His timing, His silence, or His purposes, but you begin to believe that there is meaning woven into your story deeper than the surface of your pain. This is not resignation. It is recognition. Recognition that God has been faithful in your past, present in your weakness, and attentive to every tear you have shed. And slowly, this recognition becomes the foundation for something new.

The moment hope takes root—even in tender, fragile form—you begin to notice things you were unable to see before. You notice the way someone sits a little longer beside you, even when there is nothing left to say. You notice the gentleness in the hands that help you stand. You notice the patience in the voice of the family member who answers the same question again and again without irritation. You notice the prayer someone whispers when they think you are asleep. These gestures are not small. They are love made visible in the ordinary rhythm of suffering. And hope sharpens your sight so you can finally see them for what they are.

You start to realise that your life has been surrounded—perhaps more than you knew—by people whose hearts are knit to yours. They may not know how to express their love perfectly. They may fear saying the wrong thing. They may carry their own quiet grief over what you are facing. But they are there. They walk into rooms that feel heavy. They stand beside hospital beds where silence stretches long. They show up not because they have solutions, but because love refuses to leave. Suffering often exposes what comfort hides: the depth, the loyalty, the stubbornness of love. Hope helps you recognise it.

And something else shifts. You begin to see that your suffering has not only affected you—it has drawn others into a deeper communion. Love becomes simpler. The masks fall away. Pretence disappears. Relationships become distilled to what truly matters: presence, tenderness, sacrifice, patience. There is no room left for trivialities. Illness has a way of purifying the space around you until only the essentials remain. Hope makes these essentials visible. You discover that the people who love you are not spectators standing outside your pain; they are participants in a grace that God is pouring into your story.

This realisation often brings a mixture of gratitude and fear. Gratitude, because you see how deeply you are loved. Fear, because you worry that your suffering imposes too much, asks too much, requires too much. The thought may come unbidden: *I don't want to be a burden.* Yet hope answers this fear with truth. Love does not measure cost the way fear does. Love does not tally hours or resent effort. Love does not grow smaller when it is poured out; it grows stronger. When those who love you walk with you, they are not being diminished—they are being enlarged. Suffering invites them into a part of your life that is holy ground, a place where God is at work. They do not stand there reluctantly. They stand there because grace has drawn them too.

It becomes clear, perhaps for the first time, that your illness has not isolated you; it has revealed the depth of your relationships. It has shown you who carries you, who intercedes for you, who listens even when words fail, who remains steady when the days feel uncertain. Hope allows you to see that what is happening to you is not happening in a vacuum. It has ignited love in others—love that might never have surfaced so clearly without the trial you endure. You are not watching love from afar; you are at the centre of it.

And all of this points naturally toward the next stage of the journey. If Part III helped you understand the truth of who you are and the God who holds you, Part IV helps you understand the truth of the people around you—the family, the friends, the community who walk the path with you. Hope has stabilised your heart enough to perceive their love. Now that love becomes the lens through which you continue the journey.

You will begin to see that their companionship is not accidental.

God works through the people He places near you. Their care is not merely human affection; it is the echo of His own tenderness. Their willingness to help is not pity; it is participation in the mystery of Christ who said that whatever is done for the least of His brothers and sisters is done for Him. Their constancy is not obligation; it is grace taking flesh in their lives. Hope opens your eyes to what was true all along: God's love often reaches you through the love of others.

And as this becomes clearer, a new chapter begins—one in which love becomes not only something you receive but something you recognise as holy, something that carries you, strengthens you, surrounds you, and reveals God's nearness in ways you might never have noticed before. Part IV is the story of this love: the love of family, the love expressed through care and service, the love that sees beauty in fragility, the love that is awakened by suffering rather than diminished by it. Hope has prepared the ground for it. Now love begins to grow in the open.

IV

LOVE IN THE MIDST OF CANCER

Sixteen

When Family Walks the Road With You

There are few fears heavier than the quiet worry that your suffering has become too much for the people you love. It is not usually spoken aloud. It lives in the pauses between conversations, in the apologetic tone when you ask for help, in the way your eyes drop when someone adjusts a pillow or fills a glass of water or sits beside you longer than they planned. Illness, especially cancer, awakens an ache that goes deeper than the physical: the fear that your pain is costing others more than they should have to bear. Yet love within a family does not work the way fear imagines it. Love does not weigh the burden and resent the weight. Love sees the person first, always. Love chooses presence even when the road grows hard. When family walks with you through suffering, they do not walk as victims of your pain but as participants in grace. Something sacred unfolds in them as much as in you.

Scripture shows this again and again, not as theory but as lived reality. Ruth, in one of the most tender gestures in all of Scripture, refused to abandon Naomi in her bitterness and grief. "Where you go, I will go; your people shall be my people, and your God my God" (Ruth 1:16).

Ruth was not trapped; she was drawn. Love bound her to Naomi in a way suffering only strengthened. The story does not portray Ruth as burdened, but blessed—blessed to accompany, blessed to share the road, blessed to love in a way that demanded something of her heart. Suffering created an opening through which grace flowed, and the relationship between them became deeper, purer, and more luminous because of it.

Or consider Mary standing beneath the Cross of her Son. The Gospel does not describe her as overwhelmed, nor as a passive observer crushed under the weight of another's agony. She is present—a presence so faithful that Christ, in His final hour, entrusted her to the beloved disciple and the beloved disciple to her. "Woman, behold your son ... Behold your mother" (John 19:26–27). The early Fathers saw in this moment the birth of a new kind of family, one bound not by blood alone but by love strengthened through suffering. St. Augustine said, "Love is the weight that moves the soul," meaning that true love always inclines us toward the ones who suffer, because Christ Himself has drawn near to suffering. Mary's love at the Cross was not diminished by grief; it was revealed by it. Your family's love, too, is revealed—not lessened—by the hardship they share with you.

The fear of being a burden usually comes from a misunderstanding of what love is. We often imagine that love flourishes when life is easy, when everyone is strong and independent. Yet Scripture teaches the opposite. Love matures when it carries weight. St. Paul tells the Galatians, "Bear one another's burdens, and so fulfil the law of Christ" (Galatians 6:2). He does not describe this as an act of heroism but as the ordinary rhythm of Christian life. The "law of Christ" is the law of shared suffering, mutual charity, and the quiet heroism of presence. When your family bears part of your suffering, they are not losing themselves; they are fulfilling their deepest vocation.

John Paul II understood this with remarkable clarity. In *Salvifici*

Doloris, he writes that suffering "unleashes love in the human person," because suffering creates a space where the heart can give itself more freely, more tenderly, more sacrificially. Love "unleashed" is not sentimental, nor is it abstract. It is the love that arranges blankets, drives to appointments, sits in waiting rooms, prepares meals, prays in silence, and keeps vigil during long nights. It is love that moves toward weakness, not away from it. When your family cares for you, they are not doing something small—they are entering a mystery Christ Himself revealed: the mystery of love that becomes stronger precisely when it is tested.

One of the deepest truths of the Christian faith is that God never asks us to carry our crosses alone. Jesus stumbled under His Cross—a staggering, physical, humiliating moment that revealed His full humanity. And in that moment, the Father did not send an angel to strengthen Him; He sent a man. Simon of Cyrene stepped into the story, pressed by circumstance yet transformed by grace. The Gospels do not praise Simon for his efficiency or strength; they praise the fact that he shared the burden of Christ. This is the shape of love in a suffering world: it steps forward, even when afraid, even when unsure, even when it feels unprepared. When your family carries you in small or great ways, they are living this same mystery. They are Simon. And you, by needing their help, become the place where God invites them into a deeper love than they have ever known.

It is holy—deeply, unmistakably holy—to allow others to love you. Many people imagine that holiness means strength, independence, self-sufficiency. Yet Christ Himself allowed others to care for Him. Mary held Him as an infant. Joseph protected Him as a child. Martha served Him food. Veronica wiped His face. The women at the tomb anointed His body. He let Himself be loved at every stage of His life, especially when He was weakest. If the Son of God did not consider it unworthy to receive love, neither should you. Accepting help does not diminish your dignity; it reveals it. It shows that you trust others enough to let them into the place where you are vulnerable, and trust is the foundation of all genuine love.

Your suffering does not make your family weaker. It calls forth strengths they may never have discovered otherwise. It teaches patience, compassion, tenderness, and humility. It draws them closer not only to you, but to God. In walking this road with you, they participate in a grace that will remain with them long after the suffering passes. They are learning to love with the love Christ Himself poured out on the Cross—a love willing to stand in difficult places, a love that does not flee from pain, a love that triumphs through faithfulness. St. John Chrysostom once described the Christian home as the "little Church," a sacred place where love is lived more than spoken. Your illness, painful though it is, becomes a moment when your family's "little Church" is purified, strengthened, and sanctified.

You may not see the transformation unfolding in them, but it is happening. In the quiet ways they adjust their lives, in the tenderness that was once hidden, in the patience that grows through repeated acts of care, something in them is being reshaped. They are not losing themselves; they are becoming more fully themselves. Love has this effect. It enlarges the heart through sacrifice. It teaches the soul to move beyond convenience and comfort. It awakens depths that ease and routine could never reach. Your suffering becomes a place where their love takes root, grows strong, and stretches toward God. This is not a burden you have placed upon them. It is a grace God is offering to them through you.

You may still hear a voice inside whispering that none of this can be true, that the cost is too high, that others would be happier if they did not have to walk this road with you. Pain can distort perception. Fear can cloud the truth. Yet the lives of the saints tell a different story. Whenever someone suffers, the circle of people around them becomes a field where grace works quietly but powerfully. St. Augustine taught that love "rejoices in the beloved's burden," meaning that love does not look at sacrifice with resentment but with a kind of solemn joy, because it has found a place where it can give itself fully. Your family's love for you is not weakened by the weight they carry; it is made more real, more Christlike, more eternal.

To deny them the chance to love you is to deny them the chance to grow in the very virtues that make a family holy. Love becomes sterile if it is never stretched. Compassion becomes theory if it is never exercised. Patience remains shallow if it is never tested. Holiness becomes abstract if it never enters the real world of weakness and need. When you allow your family to walk this path with you, you are not burdening them—you are inviting them to live the Gospel in its most concrete form. You are inviting them to live the words of Christ: "Whatever you did for one of the least of these, you did for me" (Matthew 25:40). In caring for you, they are touching Christ. In loving you, they are loving Him.

And there is something else—a truth quieter but no less sacred. Your vulnerability gives your family permission to be vulnerable too. When they see your courage in weakness, they learn that weakness is not shameful. When they see your faith in fear, they learn that fear is not the enemy of trust. When they see your hope in the midst of pain, they learn that hope is larger than any circumstance. Your suffering becomes a school in which everyone is taught, not by lectures but by love. You are teaching them, simply by being you, what it means to endure with dignity and to turn toward God in the midst of affliction. This is not a burden. It is a gift.

One of the greatest lies suffering whispers is, "You are alone." Yet nothing in your life has ever disproved that lie more clearly than this season. Look at the faces beside you. Look at the hands that steady you. Look at the people who rearrange their days, who show up without being asked, who call, who pray, who sit in silence because words feel too small. They are not there by accident. They are not there out of obligation. They are there because God has drawn them close. He has braided their lives with yours so tightly that your suffering has become part of their redemption as well. The love they give to you is forming their souls for eternity.

Do not fear the cost of your needs. Love is not diminished by the weight it carries; it is revealed by it. When a family walks together through suffering, the bonds between them do not fray. They deepen. Shared tears become shared strength. Shared nights of worry become shared victories of perseverance. Shared fatigue becomes shared tenderness. The family becomes, more than ever before, a living icon of the Body of Christ—many members, one heart, one love, one hope. Your suffering has not fractured your family. It has united them around something eternal.

Even now, you may think, "I wish they did not have to go through this." But they are not going through this instead of their true lives—they are going through this as the most meaningful part of their lives. They will remember these days not as days stolen from them, but as days given to them, days when love was purified, when faith became embodied, when grace entered the ordinary and made it holy. Years from now, they will speak of this time with reverence, not regret. They will say that loving you during this season changed them in ways comfort never could have. They will say that they discovered depths in themselves that only suffering could have awakened.

Let yourself be loved. Let yourself be carried when you cannot walk. Let yourself be held when the night feels long. Let yourself lean on those whom God has placed beside you. The grace that has sustained you is the same grace sustaining them. Your suffering is not only your cross; it is the place where God is shaping the people who love you. You are not a burden. You are a blessing that is forming their hearts for heaven. Through you, they are learning what it means to love as Christ loves—faithfully, tenderly, and without fear of the cost.

And as this love deepens, you will begin to see that the road ahead is not a solitary path but a shared pilgrimage. Every step you take is taken together. Every tear is caught by more than one heart. Every sigh becomes a prayer that rises not from one voice but from many. You walk with them, and they walk with you, and God walks with you all. This is the mystery unfolding in your midst: suffering has not diminished your family; it has revealed what holds you together. Love is stronger than fear, stronger than frailty, stronger than cancer. And in this love, God is nearer than your breath.

Seventeen

The Gift of Accepting Help

There comes a stage in suffering when the hardest thing is no longer the pain or the fatigue or the uncertainty of the next appointment. It is the simple, humbling realization that you need other people in ways you never did before. You used to move freely, carry groceries, climb stairs, prepare meals, drive yourself to appointments. You used to be the one who helped others. Now you find yourself leaning on arms that steady you, accepting meals you did not cook, letting someone else arrange rides or fold laundry or sit beside you because doing it alone is no longer possible. There is a tenderness in this dependency, but also a quiet ache. You may feel embarrassed by it, as though needing help has taken something from you. You may feel guilty for interrupting the routines of your family. You may marvel at how quickly illness changes the balance of daily life. And beneath all these feelings, perhaps without saying it aloud, there is a fear: "I don't want to be a burden."

This fear is older than you. It runs deep in the human heart. We like to imagine ourselves as self-sufficient. We like to give, not receive. We feel comfortable offering help, but uneasy when the roles are reversed.

Yet Scripture reveals something subtle but profound: the very refusal to receive help was never part of God's design for the human person. In the beginning, God did not create one solitary figure who needed no one. He said, "It is not good that the man should be alone" (Genesis 2:18). This was not simply a comment about marriage. It was a declaration about human nature. We are made to live in communion. We are made to need and to be needed. We are fashioned by God as people who flourish through relationship, through shared strength, through mutual care. Dependency is not a flaw in the design. It is part of the design.

But suffering magnifies this truth in ways we would never have chosen. Illness forces us to confront the limits we once ignored. Cancer does not ask permission to weaken the body. It does not apologize for the days when the smallest task requires more effort than you possess. And when weakness appears, the temptation is to assume that something essential about your dignity has been diminished. Yet the pattern of the Gospel points in an entirely different direction. The moment that reveals your need is the moment that reveals God's heart.

The clearest example, the one that shines with quiet boldness on the pages of the Gospels, appears on the road to Calvary. As Jesus carries His Cross through the narrow streets of Jerusalem, the weight crushes His wounded body. The crowd presses in. The soldiers grow impatient. And then the evangelists tell us something astonishing: "They compelled a passerby, Simon of Cyrene, to carry His Cross" (Mark 15:21). This is not a decorative detail. This is revelation. The Son of God, who healed the blind and raised the dead, who calmed storms with a word, who walked on water and cast out demons, does not walk to Calvary alone. He accepts the help of another man. The One who carried the sins of the world lets someone else carry the wood that symbolized the world's salvation.

Meditate on that for a moment: Christ allowed Himself to be helped.

He was not pretending to be tired. He was not staging a spiritual lesson. He was exhausted. His body was collapsing. And in that moment, the incarnate God permitted Simon's strength to enter His weakness. The humility of Jesus was not limited to His birth in a manger; it extended to the path of suffering where He allowed a stranger to place his shoulder under the Cross. The Church Fathers never overlooked this moment. St. Augustine wrote that in Simon's help we see "the fellowship of the redeemed," that Christ "receives as brotherly what He has given as divine." St. John Chrysostom saw it as the embodiment of Galatians 6:2: "Bear one another's burdens, and so fulfill the law of Christ." Before St. Paul ever penned those words, Christ had lived them.

This single moment redefines the fear of being a burden. If Jesus accepted help, then receiving help is not shameful. It is Christlike. It is an imitation of the humility of the Son of God. Your need does not distance you from Him; it draws you into the very mystery of His own self-emptying love. As St. Paul says in Philippians, "He emptied Himself, taking the form of a servant... He humbled Himself" (Philippians 2:7-8). And that humility included the willingness to let another human being steady Him.

Cancer may require a similar humility from you. Not because you have failed, but because you are walking a road where your strength cannot carry you alone. The body grows tired. The mind grows heavy. Tasks that once demanded no thought now ask more from you than you can give. And the enemy whispers: "You should be doing more. You should be stronger. You shouldn't need this much help." But those whispers are lies. They do not come from God. Scripture counters them with a gentler truth: "We, who are many, are one body in Christ, and individually members of one another" (Romans 12:5). To belong to Christ is to belong to His Body, and the Body does not consider its weaker members a burden. It considers them precious.

Your family does not see you as a burden. They see you as someone they love. They do not help you reluctantly. They help you because their hearts will not let them do otherwise. Love is not weakened by sacrifice; it is strengthened by it. When you let your son or daughter or sibling or spouse lift a weight you can no longer carry, you give them the sacred gift of participating in your suffering. This is not pity. This is communion. It is the deep spiritual truth John Paul II described in *Salvifici Doloris*, when he wrote that suffering "is present in order to unleash love." When you allow another person to help you, you are unleashing love in them. You are giving them a place to pour their tenderness, their patience, their devotion, their courage. Your vulnerability becomes their vocation. Your weakness becomes their offering.

This is why accepting help is not an act of defeat. It is an act of generosity. It allows others to grow in compassion, to imitate Christ, to live out the command to "love one another as I have loved you" (John 13:34). When someone you love carries your burden, they are not losing anything. They are discovering the depth of their own capacity to love. They are entering the mystery that St. Augustine described when he said, "Let us help one another in our weaknesses, for together we are strong." In the early Church, strength was never measured by independence. Strength was measured by communion — by the willingness to share life and suffering and responsibility together.

Sickness reveals this truth with painful clarity. It shows how interwoven our lives really are. It dismantles the illusion of self-sufficiency. It reminds us that human dignity does not depend on what we can do, but on who we are. And who you are has not changed. You are still the beloved of the Father. You are still a temple of the Holy Spirit. You are still the image of God. Your value is not reduced by the limitations of your body. If anything, suffering reveals the depth of your soul in ways that were hidden during days of strength.

It takes courage to let others see your weakness. It takes even greater courage to let them enter it. Yet God does something holy in that exchange. When someone sits beside you during a treatment, when they kneel to tie your shoes because bending hurts too much, when they carry the laundry basket because you no longer can, when they steady your arm as you walk from the bed to the bathroom, they are not witnessing your loss of dignity — they are witnessing your trust. And trust is never undignified. Trust is grace in motion.

Think of how children trust their parents. The child who lifts her arms to be carried is not ashamed of her need. Her dependency is not a burden; it is a bond. She is most herself when she rests in the strength of another. Jesus Himself points to children as icons of the Kingdom: "Whoever does not receive the kingdom of God like a child shall not enter it" (Mark 10:15). He is telling us that the spiritual life is not a climb toward self-reliance. It is a surrender into the Father's care. When illness pushes you into a posture of childlike trust, you are not regressing. You are growing into the shape of the Gospel. You are living the beatitude of the poor in spirit, the blessed ones who know they must lean on God in every breath.

This is why the Fathers often spoke of suffering as a kind of purification — not a punishment, but a revelation. St. Gregory the Great said that suffering "opens the ear of the heart," making us attentive to graces we could not hear before. And often what we hear most clearly in suffering is the voice of God speaking through the love of others. When someone helps you bathe, or prepares food, or sits in silence beside you when words feel heavy, God is not absent from that moment. He is within it. The love you receive is the love He is giving. The gentleness shown to you is His gentleness. The hands that support you echo the hands of Christ who promised, "I am with you always, even to the end of the age" (Matthew 28:20).

Yet you may still feel the quiet guilt of being the one who needs instead of the one who gives. You may wonder whether the weight you place on others is too heavy. But remember: love always bends itself toward the one who is suffering. Love delights in self-gift. The entire Christian mystery is built upon the truth that love reveals itself most fully when it bears the burden of another. Christ does not love us from a distance. He enters our weakness. He carries our sins. He touches lepers, consoles mourners, lifts the fallen, and lets a Cyrenian shoulder His Cross. To accept help is to let others imitate Him.

Sometimes the deepest grace comes not from doing but from allowing. Allowing yourself to be helped is a form of humility that unites your suffering with Christ's. It strips away the illusion that we stand alone. It roots you in the communion of the Church. It teaches those who love you the sacred tenderness of sacrifice. And it allows relationships to deepen in ways they never could when you were strong. Illness changes the patterns of daily life, but it can also reveal a kindness in others that astonishes you. People who once seemed busy become gentle. Those who struggled to express affection suddenly find the language of touch, presence, service. They discover in themselves a capacity for devotion they never knew they had. Your suffering becomes the door through which their love walks freely.

This is part of the mystery St. Paul names when he says, "If one member suffers, all suffer together" (1 Corinthians 12:26). He does not say this as poetry. He says it as reality. The Church is a body, and your suffering is not suffering in isolation. When you are weak, the other members compensate. When you cannot stand, others rise. When you cannot pray, others intercede. When you cannot carry your own weight, the Body carries you. The Christian life was never meant to be lived as isolated individuals. It was meant to be lived as shared life, shared strength, shared wounds.

Your willingness to receive help teaches the people around you how to love more fully. It teaches them compassion, patience, humility, and solidarity. It teaches them that love is not measured by convenience but by faithfulness. And in this exchange, something remarkable occurs: both you and the ones helping you are drawn closer to Christ. They see Christ in you — in your vulnerability, your trust, your endurance. And you see Christ in them — in their service, their generosity, their quiet acts of mercy. In receiving their help, you become a living icon of the suffering Christ; in giving you help, they become icons of the Christ who comforts and carries.

Do not underestimate the spiritual weight of these small daily interactions. They are not distractions from the spiritual life. They are the spiritual life. John Paul II wrote that in suffering we discover "the highest calling of love," and this calling unfolds not only in heroic acts but in the simple movements of care and dependency. Illness teaches us that holiness is not reserved for extraordinary moments; it is revealed in the tenderness shared between those who suffer and those who love them.

This means that your dependency is not a detour from your dignity. It is part of the path God is shaping within you. He is inviting you to receive love in a way that mirrors how He receives the devotion of His children. He is inviting you to rest in the strength of others the way we all rest in His. He is inviting you to discover that your worth is not tied to what you can accomplish, but to who you are — a beloved child, held in the embrace of a Father who never grows weary of caring for you.

Let go, then, of the fear that accepting help diminishes you. It does not. It ennobles you. It reveals the humility of Christ at work within you. It allows the people who love you to become living participants in your journey. And it draws you into the deeper communion that God intended from the beginning — a communion where no one carries their burden alone, and where every act of shared weakness becomes a revelation of divine love.

Illness may ask you to surrender many things, but it never asks you to surrender your dignity. Your dignity is held by God, and God cannot lose what He holds. To accept help is to place yourself safely within the arms of love — human love, yes, but also the eternal love that beats in every heart that lifts, supports, or walks beside you. In this way your need becomes sacramental. It reveals the invisible grace of the One who carried His Cross with Simon beside Him, and who now carries you with the people He has placed around your life. Your willingness to receive is not weakness; it is a participation in the humility of Christ. And in that humility, something beautiful unfolds: you become the place where love learns how to love more deeply.

Your dependency is sacred. It is not the breaking of your dignity but the widening of it. It is the space where communion grows, where hearts are shaped, where God's tenderness finds flesh, and where the quiet glory of carrying one another becomes the clearest sign that Christ is still among us.

Eighteen

How Your Suffering Touches Others

There is a quiet truth about suffering that few people ever see from the inside: you rarely recognize the impact your suffering has on the people around you. When you are the one in pain, the one walking through treatments, the one enduring sleepless nights and long appointments and the heavy silence of uncertainty, your world grows smaller. You feel the limits of your strength, the uncertainty of your body, the narrowing of your days. You see what is difficult, what has been taken from you, what is now beyond your reach. But the people watching you—your family, your friends, your nurses, your doctors, even strangers—see something else. They see courage you do not feel. They see patience you do not recognize. They see faith that looks stronger than you think it is. They see love ripening under the weight of suffering. They see grace shining through the cracks of weakness. And without ever intending it, without ever trying, you begin to change them.

This is one of the hidden mysteries of suffering: its radiance. Not a radiance that denies pain or erases sorrow, but a radiance that emerges precisely through them. Saint Paul wrote from prison—his body chained, his ministry interrupted, his plans shattered—that "most of the brothers, having become confident in the Lord by my imprisonment, are much more bold to speak the word without fear" (Philippians 1:14). Paul did not feel strong. He did not feel inspirational. He felt confined, wounded, limited. Yet it was *his limitation* that set others free. His suffering became a kind of fire in the early Church, illuminating courage in those who watched him endure it.

Something similar happens around every person walking through cancer. You may not notice it, because suffering turns your gaze inward. But others notice. They see the way you keep moving forward, one small step at a time. They notice that you still greet people with gentleness, even on days when your whole body aches. They see you sit in waiting rooms without bitterness. They see how fiercely you love your family, how determined you are to finish each day with dignity. They see the way you hold onto God—not always triumphantly, sometimes only by a thread—but that thread inspires them more than the strongest sermon they have ever heard.

God works through this in ways you cannot imagine. Suffering is never wasted because love is never wasted. John Paul II wrote in *Salvifici Doloris* that suffering "unleashes love in the human community," and he meant it literally. Your suffering has become a place where love is awakened in others. People pray who have not prayed in years. Families reconcile. Children soften. Friends return. Nurses linger a little longer in your hospital room, drawn by something they cannot name. Even those who barely know you begin to carry you in their hearts. Your suffering becomes a quiet ministry—not the ministry of words, but the ministry of witness, the ministry of endurance, the ministry of trust.

This is the pattern woven throughout Scripture. Think of Job. He did not know that in his lamentations, in his honest cries to God, he was silencing Satan himself. He did not know that his perseverance would become a model for countless generations. Job was not trying to inspire anyone. He was simply trying to survive. Yet heaven and earth were watching, and his suffering became a revelation of fidelity that echoed far beyond his own lifetime.

Or consider the mother in 2 Maccabees who watched her seven sons die rather than deny their faith. She did not feel brave; she endured unimaginable agony. Yet her courage strengthened her sons. Her suffering became the spark that ignited their martyrdom. Scripture says, "She encouraged each of them in the language of their fathers" (2 Maccabees 7:21), not through eloquence but through the force of love that radiated from her anguish.

But nowhere is this mystery clearer than at the foot of the Cross. Mary stood there in silence, her heart pierced, her Son dying before her eyes. She spoke no speeches. She performed no miracles. She simply endured. And her endurance became a source of strength for the Church from that moment until now. The Cross transformed the world not only through Christ's suffering, but through the suffering of those who loved Him. Love made their suffering luminous.

Your suffering carries a similar hidden light. People who watch you endure cancer learn what love looks like when it is tested. They learn what hope looks like when there is no certainty. They learn what patience looks like when every nerve screams for relief. They learn what faith looks like when prayers seem unanswered. You are teaching them, without even knowing it, that the human heart is capable of greatness even when the body is frail.

This is why Chrysostom called suffering "a hidden martyrdom," a witness offered not in arenas but in hospital rooms, living rooms, and sleepless nights. He said that those who suffer with faith "preach Christ even when they are silent." You may feel that your days have grown small, that your world has become narrow, but in God's eyes your witness has never been greater. Every moment you persevere becomes a seed planted in the souls of others—seeds you will not see bloom, but seeds that heaven cherishes.

People change when they see someone suffer with trust. They soften. They examine their own priorities. They pray more deeply. They become gentler with their own families. They rediscover compassion. Your presence becomes a mirror in which they see their lives differently. Not because you set out to teach them anything, but because suffering has a clarity that comfort never provides. Suffering strips life down to what matters, and the people who love you cannot help but be drawn into that clarity.

Even your moments of weakness, your tears, your frustrations, your fears—these too have their impact. When people see you struggle honestly, they gain the courage to face their own struggles without shame. When they see you cling to God with questions rather than certainties, they learn that faith is not about having all the answers; it is about staying with God even in the dark. Augustine once wrote that God uses "the suffering of the righteous to instruct the hearts of both the strong and the weak," and he meant that even the honest trembling of a suffering soul has a sanctifying effect on the community around them.

You may not realize it, but your suffering has already changed the shape of the days of those who love you. They wake up thinking of you. They pray without being asked. They arrange their schedules. They bring meals. They send messages. They sit with you in silence. They remember what it means to love with their whole hearts. In a world obsessed with noise and comfort and distraction, your suffering has become a place where they remember who they truly are.

And there is more. Suffering can deepen love in those around you beyond anything they have known before. When someone helps you stand, or steadies your arm, or changes your bandage, or waits for you at a doctor's office, they are not simply performing a task. They are learning what real love costs—and discovering that it is worth everything. Love that serves the suffering becomes more tender, more patient, more Christlike. In the Gospels, the people who touched Jesus in His moments of need were transformed by Him, but those who tended to Him—Mary, John, Veronica, Simon—were also transformed. The Cross changed them because love always transforms the one who offers it.

And this transformation continues now through your life. When someone helps you settle into bed, or holds your hand during a difficult moment, or speaks to you softly when you feel afraid, something holy is happening in them. They are being shaped by your suffering into people who love more deeply than they once knew how. They are discovering a compassion that lies dormant in most people until they encounter someone they cannot help but love. They are becoming gentler, wiser, more patient, more selfless. Your suffering becomes the place where their goodness awakens. You may feel like you are the one being carried, but in carrying you, they are learning the weight of love. God is forming their hearts through your weakness.

And even beyond this visible circle—your family, your closest friends—your suffering touches others you may never meet. Nurses enter rooms every day, but some patients remain with them long after their shifts end. You may not see it, but your strength, your gratitude, your quiet endurance stays with them. Doctors feel the difference when they meet a patient who carries pain without bitterness. Other patients notice the way you smile at them, or greet them, or simply sit beside them in the waiting room. The suffering of Christians has always had an apostolic character, not because it is loud, but because it is real. People trust authenticity. When they see someone cling to God in the middle of hardship, they feel invited—quietly, gently—to reconsider their own relationship with Him.

Christians in the early Church often spoke of suffering as "the seed of faith" in others. Nothing persuaded the world of the truth of the Gospel more than seeing believers endure trials with a grace that seemed larger than themselves. Tertullian famously wrote, "The blood of martyrs is the seed of the Church," but this principle is not limited to martyrdom. Every suffering borne with love becomes a seed. Some seeds blossom into conversions. Some blossom into deeper prayer. Some blossom into hidden virtues. You may never see what blossoms from your suffering, but God sees it. Heaven watches the harvest grow in places your eyes cannot yet reach.

This is why suffering is never solitary, even when it feels that way. It sends ripples into the lives of others. Sometimes those ripples are subtle: a friend becomes more patient with her children because your patience has humbled her; a spouse apologizes more quickly because he sees how short life is; a sibling prays for the first time in years; a grandchild asks questions about heaven; a neighbour leaves a meal on your doorstep because they remember the fragility of life. These acts may seem small, but God builds His Kingdom out of the small things. Love grows quietly, like yeast in dough. Your suffering becomes the leaven.

Yet perhaps the most mysterious and beautiful way your suffering touches others is in its ability to summon love out of them without force. No one can watch someone they love suffer without being changed. Love is called forth in moments of vulnerability. It deepens, purifies, matures. People who once felt awkward expressing affection suddenly find themselves saying things they never said before. Old grievances lose their power. Priorities rearrange. The heart softens. This is not accidental. This is grace. This is God ministering to others through your life.

Saint Paul says, "We have this treasure in jars of clay, to show that the surpassing power belongs to God and not to us" (2 Corinthians 4:7).

Illness makes the clay fragile. It shows the cracks. But the treasure—the life of Christ within you—shines through the cracks more brilliantly than through any polished strength. People encounter God not despite your weakness, but through it. They see something in you that they cannot name, something that steadies them, something that draws them to pray, something that makes them want to love better. You may feel emptied, but others see you overflowing with a grace you do not feel.

Do not underestimate the holiness of what you are offering to the world simply by continuing to love, to trust, to endure. You are offering a witness stronger than anything you could have offered in health. In health, people might admire your accomplishments. In sickness, they encounter your soul. In health, people might respect your strength. In sickness, they encounter your faith. In health, people might look up to you. In sickness, they look into themselves and ask, "What truly matters?"

Your suffering is not passive. It is active. It is not meaningless. It is sacramental. God is using your life—your real, fragile, complicated, beautiful life—to soften hearts, open eyes, awaken compassion, deepen faith, and build communion. You are not only being carried; you are carrying others in ways you cannot yet see.

And this is why your suffering is not the end of your vocation. It is an expansion of it. You are not less fruitful now. You are, in many ways, more fruitful than ever. Christ does His greatest work through people who feel weakest. Saint Paul heard Him say, "My power is made perfect in weakness" (2 Corinthians 12:9). This was not a poetic sentiment. It was an explanation of how God transforms suffering into grace. The weaker the vessel, the more clearly the power of God shines through it.

One day—perhaps not in this life, perhaps only in the life to come—you will see all the people who were changed because of your suffering.

You will meet them in the light of God. You will hear the stories. You will understand the invisible ripples of grace. You will see the prayers awakened, the hearts softened, the relationships restored, the faith ignited. You will see the full tapestry of love God wove through your pain. And you will understand that nothing, not one tear, not one sigh, not one night of anguish, was wasted.

But until that day comes, take comfort in this: you are not simply enduring cancer. You are ministering through it. You are revealing Christ to others. You are teaching love without speaking a word. You are living a hidden vocation that touches more lives than you know. And the God who sees in secret sees the beauty of your offering. Your suffering is not only shaping you. It is shaping the world around you, quietly, profoundly, tenderly. It is touching others in ways only heaven can fully measure.

Nineteen

Where Earthly Love Meets Eternal Hope

There is a moment in every journey through suffering when you begin to understand that love has been carrying you in ways you could not see at first. Part IV has walked through that hidden territory—where family draws close, where help becomes holy, where your own weakness becomes a place where others discover their strength, and where your suffering quietly shapes the hearts around you. You may not have noticed it in the beginning, because pain turns the gaze inward, and fatigue narrows the world to the next hour, the next appointment, the next breath. But as the days unfold, a strange truth emerges: you have not been walking through this alone, and you have not been walking through this untouched. Love has been working in you, and through you, and even around you in ways you never expected.

You have seen your family walk beside you—sometimes with confidence, sometimes with trembling, sometimes with more love than words can express. You have seen how suffering draws out a tenderness that daily life often hides. You have seen how relationships deepen when one person is hurting and the others cannot bear to let them hurt alone. You have watched love rearrange itself: priorities shifting, schedules bending, ordinary tasks becoming acts of devotion. And you have discovered that letting yourself be loved is not a burden to those who care for you—it is a grace that enlarges their hearts.

You have learned that accepting help is not a mark of defeat but a mark of Christ. The same Christ who healed the sick and raised the dead also let Simon of Cyrene carry His Cross. He, who needed nothing, allowed Himself to be helped by someone who did not even know Him. He did this so that no one who is weak would ever feel ashamed of being carried. He sanctified dependence. He turned the receiving of help into an act of humility that mirrors divine love. When you let others help you, you are not stepping away from Christ—you are stepping into His footsteps on the road to Calvary.

And perhaps most surprisingly, you have begun to see—or at least to sense—that your suffering has not only shaped you but has been shaping others. Not through speeches, not through displays of strength, but through the fragile, honest way you have continued to trust, continued to endure, continued to love. Suffering has a mysterious way of revealing what matters most, not only to the one who suffers but to everyone who stands close enough to see. The patience you didn't know you had, the courage you thought you lacked, the prayers you whispered in fear—these things have touched hearts in ways you may never fully comprehend. You have become, without intending it, a witness. A teacher. A place where others encounter the love of God made visible in human frailty.

Part IV has been about this: the holiness of relationships under the weight of suffering. It has shown that the bonds between you and those who love you have not weakened—they have deepened. It has shown that your dignity has not diminished—it has become more radiant. It has shown that your suffering is not a closed room but an open door where others step in and discover who they truly are. Love has not been erased by your pain. Love has been revealed by it.

But the journey does not end here. There is another horizon rising. The love discovered in suffering begins to open toward something even greater—something that does not depend on strength or weakness, on time or circumstance, on the fragility of the body or the uncertainty of tomorrow. The love that has carried you through the hardest moments is a sign of a love even deeper, a love that does not waver, a love that suffering cannot dim and death cannot silence. You have seen love in its earthly form; now Part V turns you toward love in its eternal fullness.

Up to this point, the book has remained close to the ground—close to your experience, close to the daily realities of illness, close to the people who walk with you. It has spoken of how God meets you in the valley, in silence, in weakness, in prayer, in the long nights, in the hands and hearts of those who love you. But now the gaze begins to lift. Not away from the suffering—Christ never turns His eyes away from those who suffer—but through it, beyond it, toward the truth that suffering does not have the final word.

Part V is the turning of the page from endurance to promise, from the present struggle to the future glory, from the wounds you carry to the wounds Christ carries in His risen body. These next chapters will not deny your pain. They will not rush you to easy consolation. They will, instead, place your suffering within the great story of Christ Himself—the Christ who carried a Cross, who bore wounds, who entered death, and who rose with those wounds transformed. They will show you that the story of your life cannot be understood only in the light of what hurts now, but in the light of what God is preparing.

The first step into this new horizon is the Resurrection—not as a distant doctrine, not as a story you learned long ago, but as a hope meant for you personally. Christ rose with His wounds, and that detail is not accidental. The Gospels make a point of it. The Risen Lord tells Thomas, "Put your finger here, and see My hands" (John 20:27). The wounds did not disappear. They were not erased. They were glorified. This is the mystery that will open Part V: that God does not discard what has hurt you. He transforms it. Your wounds, like His, can become radiant in ways you cannot yet imagine.

From there, the journey will move toward the truth that suffering—and even death—cannot touch what is deepest in you. The body weakens, but the soul remains held. Identity remains anchored. You remain the one God loves, the one God formed, the one God will never abandon. Cancer can take much from you, but it cannot claim the core of who you are. You are more than your diagnosis. You are more than your fears. You are more than the limits of your strength. You are a child of the Father, and nothing—not even death—can take that away.

And finally, Part V will lead you gently into the mystery of healing—not as a single outcome, not as a guarantee of earthly cure, but as a promise that God heals in more ways than one. Some healing happens in the body. Some happens in the heart. And some happens in eternity, where Christ has prepared a place where suffering is no more. Healing is never wasted. Prayer is never ignored. Death is not defeat for those who belong to the One who has already walked into death and emerged victorious.

Part IV has shown you how deeply you are loved in the midst of suffering. Part V will show you how deeply you are loved beyond it. When you turn the page, you are stepping into the great Christian hope: that the story does not end with cancer, or fear, or weakness, or even death. The story ends in the hands of the God who makes all things new.

V

THE STORY DOES NOT END HERE

Twenty

The Resurrection and the Wounds That Shine

When the risen Christ entered the locked room where the disciples hid in fear, He did not begin with explanations or grand declarations. He began by showing them His hands. Before He spoke of mission or forgiveness or peace, He allowed them to see the marks of the nails, the places where suffering had entered His flesh. The Gospel tells us that "He showed them His hands and His side," and only then "the disciples were glad when they saw the Lord" (John 20:19–20). It is striking that this is the first revelation of the Resurrection: not a display of dazzling power, but a Savior whose glorified body still carries the wounds of love. The very same hands that once gripped the wood of the Cross now radiated the light of a life death could no longer touch. Yet the scars remained. The risen Lord did not hide them, did not explain them away, did not smooth them over as though they belonged to a story concluded. Instead, He carried them into eternity as trophies of the victory His love had won.

The Fathers of the Church never tired of contemplating this mystery.

Augustine said the wounds were "beautiful" in the Resurrection, because they were no longer signs of pain but signs of love's endurance. Gregory the Great wrote that Christ kept His scars so that "He might heal the wounds of our unbelief," as though the very things that once caused fear had become instruments of faith. Thomas Aquinas added that the scars remain for "glory, testimony, and joy"—glory for Christ, testimony for the world, joy for the redeemed. The wounds no longer bleed, no longer ache, no longer mark humiliation. They shine. They proclaim that nothing offered in love is ever lost, that God wastes nothing, that sacrifice is not swallowed by death but sown into eternal life.

This is the truth that speaks most powerfully to anyone who suffers, especially to those whose bodies carry scars they never wished for. Cancer can mark a person in ways that feel harsh and undeserved—scars from surgery that make a mirror feel unfamiliar, changes from treatment that reshape the sense of self, the quiet ache of knowing that the body once taken for granted now limps through each day. Yet the risen Christ stands before the world with wounded hands, and in doing so He dignifies every wound His children bear. He reveals that God sees every mark, every place of fragility, every region of fear, and does not recoil from them. If the Son of God carries His wounds into glory, then no suffering offered to Him will fade into meaninglessness. Your scars, too—seen or unseen—are destined for transformation.

When Jesus invited Thomas to touch His wounds, He was not merely proving a point. He was revealing the intimacy of redemption. "Put your finger here," He said (John 20:27). He allowed a human hand to enter the place where sorrow had passed through His flesh. In that moment, Christ taught that the wounds of God are not closed to His people, and by extension, the wounds of His people are not closed to God. Thomas reached forward trembling, and what he touched was no longer an opening of agony but a doorway into faith. The Risen One does not shield His pain from humanity; He opens it so that humanity may find healing in Him. The God who rose is the God who remains close to every place where suffering once lived.

Your own wounds, especially those inflicted by illness, may feel like evidence of loss, of diminishment, of weakness. But in the light of the Resurrection, they become something far different. They become places where Christ has met you. They become the ground where love has fought its battles. They become the testimony of a life that has endured in faith. The Resurrection declares that, just as Christ's wounds shine with glory, your wounds—held within His—are destined not for shame but for transfiguration. You may not yet see what this means. You may not yet feel anything luminous in them. Yet neither did the disciples understand at first. Still Christ held out His hands until joy began to dawn in their hearts.

The promise of the Resurrection reaches beyond the emotional comfort of this truth and touches the very reality of the body itself. Christ rose in the body that had died, the same body that bore the nails, the same body that lay in the tomb. It was transformed, yes— radiant, incorruptible, free from suffering—but it was unmistakably His. This is why He asked for food and ate in front of the disciples, grounding their hope not in imagination but in reality. And this is why the Church teaches that your own body—this very body you inhabit now, the one that grows tired, the one that aches, the one physicians fight so hard to heal—will be raised. John Paul II once said that the Resurrection reveals the full meaning of the human body: it is created for glory, not decay; for communion, not isolation; for life without end, not life struggling against the shadow of death. The Catholic faith does not promise that you will become something other than yourself. It promises that you will become yourself perfectly.

Your identity is not undone by illness. Your dignity is not eroded by weakness. Even now, even here, in a body that may feel like it is losing strength day by day, the promise of God remains untouched: "I will raise him up on the last day" (John 6:40). Those are the words of Christ Himself. They are the anchor for a heart afraid of the future. They are the assurance for a mind that wonders what lies ahead. They are the steady truth for a soul wrestling with uncertainty. In the Resurrection of Jesus, God has already dealt with the very things you fear most. He has already entered death. He has already shattered it. He already holds the keys of life and death in His hands (Revelation 1:18). Nothing you fear surprises Him. Nothing you fear remains unconquered by Him.

This is why Christian hope is so different from mere optimism. Optimism looks for improvement; hope looks at a tomb and sees it empty. Optimism says things might get better; hope says Christ has already gone ahead of you into every dark place you fear. Optimism depends on circumstances; hope depends on the faithfulness of God. When illness raises questions about the future, hope answers not with predictions but with a Person. The living Christ stands at the centre of every fear, saying, "Do not be afraid." Not because everything will unfold according to our plans, but because everything now unfolds within His victory.

To stand before the risen Christ is to stand before the truth that love is stronger than death. Paul proclaimed that if Christ has not been raised, "your faith is in vain" (1 Corinthians 15:14). But Christ *has* been raised, and because of this, your faith is not a fragile sentiment but a share in a victory that has already shattered the grave. Even now, as you carry the weight of illness, you stand inside a story in which death does not have the last word. Your life is anchored not in the shifting sands of medical outcomes, but in the unshakeable reality that the One who loves you has conquered the grave.

This truth does not make your suffering disappear. It does not erase fear, or fatigue, or the exhaustion that treatment brings. Christ did not rise by erasing His wounds. He rose carrying them, glorified. This matters. It means that suffering offered to God—every tear, every sleepless night, every moment of pain carried with faith—enters the mystery of Christ's own suffering and rises with Him into something eternal. Your suffering is not swallowed by the darkness. It is taken up into the light. The Resurrection declares that nothing offered in love remains buried. It becomes seed. It becomes fruit. It becomes part of a harvest the world cannot see and the soul cannot yet imagine.

Many people, when faced with illness, fear that their life has been reduced to weakness or limitation. But the Gospel reveals something astonishing: the moments of greatest glory in Christ's life were not moments of earthly strength but moments of love poured out through suffering. The Cross was not the failure of His mission; it was its fulfillment. John tells us that Jesus, in His final hour, knew "that His hour had come to depart out of this world to the Father" and that "having loved His own who were in the world, He loved them to the end" (John 13:1). The Resurrection does not erase that love; it unveils what that love accomplished.

This means that your life is not measured by how strong your body feels, or by how many tasks you can complete, or by how pain-free your days are. Your life is measured by the love that remains within you, and that love is untouched by cancer. Even now, especially now, Christ shapes your heart into something that shares more deeply in His own. The weakness you feel is not a sign that you are drifting further from God. It is the very place where He draws close.

Think of the disciples on the road to Emmaus. They walked with Christ while blind to His identity, weighed down by sorrow, unable to understand the meaning of the Cross. Yet their hearts burned within them as He opened the Scriptures (Luke 24:32). They did not realize that resurrection light already surrounded them. Only later, in the breaking of the bread, did they recognize Him. Your journey through illness can feel similar: Christ walks beside you quietly, illuminating your path in ways you may not detect until later. Grace often works this way—not with spectacle, but with steady presence.

And just as Christ walked patiently with them, He walks with you. He does not hurry you through your questions. He does not shame your sadness. He does not demand that you rise above your suffering. He accompanies you. He breaks open the meaning of your experience in ways you may not fully perceive yet, but which will come to fullness in time. Every step you take—slow, painful, or uncertain—becomes part of a journey He has already walked and redeemed.

The Resurrection also speaks to the fear of what lies ahead. Fear of decline. Fear of loss. Fear of death. These fears are real, and the Gospel never mocks them. But the Gospel answers them with something stronger: the promise that the One who calls you beloved has already stepped into the grave and filled it with His own presence. Hans Urs von Balthasar once wrote that Christ descended into death so completely that "there is no night into which He has not gone ahead of us." This means there is no fear you can face that Christ has not already filled with His light.

If the Resurrection assures us of anything, it is this: death is not a wall; it is a doorway Christ has unlocked from the inside. He does not stand on the far side calling you across a chasm. He stands in the middle, holding the door open, saying, "Where I am, there you will be also" (John 14:3). That promise is not poetic comfort; it is the centre of the Christian faith. The God who took on flesh does not abandon the flesh. He raises it. He exalts it. He crowns it with glory. And because He became like us, we will become like Him—not floating spirits, not fading memories, but redeemed bodies shining with the same immortal life that pulses through His risen flesh.

The suffering you endure now is not preparation for annihilation. It is preparation for transformation. Scripture calls this transformation a "weight of glory beyond all comparison" (2 Corinthians 4:17), and Paul insists this glory grows *through* our afflictions, not apart from them. This does not mean God delights in your pain. It means God refuses to let your pain be empty. He refuses to let cancer be the author of your story. He reclaims every moment of suffering and writes it into His own narrative of redemption. One day, you will look upon His face and see that nothing was wasted—not a tear, not a fear, not a long night, not a quiet prayer whispered when your strength was gone.

This is why the Resurrection matters so profoundly in illness: it tells you what your future actually looks like. You are not moving toward darkness; you are moving toward dawn. You are not moving toward erasure; you are moving toward fulfillment. You are not moving toward abandonment; you are moving toward the embrace of the Father who has been waiting since the day you were conceived. Even your wounds—especially the deepest ones—will not be removed as though they never existed. They will be transfigured. In Christ's risen body, wounds become windows through which the glory of God shines. In your risen body, every place where love met suffering will shine with a radiance that tells the story of how God carried you.

Think of that moment, hinted at in Scripture but promised with certainty:

the moment when Christ calls your name with a tenderness beyond imagining;

the moment when your body rises, whole and strong;

the moment when every sorrow you carried is lifted;

the moment when you see, with perfect clarity, how faithful God has been.

This is not fantasy. It is the promise of the One who said, "Because I live, you also will live" (John 14:19). The Resurrection is not simply an event; it is your destiny. The glorified Christ is not merely a figure to admire; He is the pattern for your life, the shape of your future, the guarantee that cancer does not write the final line.

Even now—especially now—you can take hold of that hope. It does not require emotional strength. It does not require certainty. It does not require the absence of fear. Hope requires only this: the willingness to let Christ step into your suffering and show you His hands. The willingness to let the light of the empty tomb fall gently across the fears you carry. The willingness to say, even in weakness, "Lord, remember me." And He does. He always does.

You may feel fragile. You may feel tired. You may wonder what lies ahead. Yet the risen Christ stands beside you, wounds shining, speaking the same words He spoke to the apostles on the day everything changed:

"Peace be with you."

It is not a peace based on outcomes. It is a peace grounded in victory. His victory. A victory that already belongs to you.

Your story is not ending. Your story is being folded into the great story God has been writing since the dawn of creation—a story in which every wound can shine, every sorrow can be redeemed, and every life entrusted to Christ will be raised in glory. That is the truth the Resurrection hands to you like a gift. A truth strong enough to carry you through every fear, and gentle enough to rest beside you in every moment of weakness.

This is the hope no illness can silence.

This is the promise no suffering can erase.

This is the future that already belongs to you in Christ:

a future where the wounds you carry now will one day shine with the radiance of love fulfilled.

Twenty-One

What Death Cannot Touch

There is a fear that slips into the heart whenever illness lingers long enough for mortality to make itself known. It is not the dramatic fear of cinematic moments; it is quieter, more human, more honest. It surfaces in the pauses between medical appointments, in the stillness of hospital rooms, in the nights when the mind races ahead to futures not yet lived. Scripture never treats this fear as weakness. The Psalms speak of hearts fainting, bones trembling, souls overwhelmed. Hebrews says humanity lives "in lifelong bondage" to the fear of death until Christ frees us (Hebrews 2:15). Even Jesus allowed the nearness of death to weigh upon His soul, saying, "My heart is sorrowful, even to death" (Mark 14:34). Fear of mortality is not a failure of faith; it is part of being human. Faith does not silence this fear. Faith places that fear into the hands of the Father.

Illness has a way of pushing the question of mortality into sharper relief. The mind begins to wonder: *What will become of me? What will happen to the ones I love? What lies beyond the veil? Will I still be myself? Will God be there?* These questions do not mean you are losing faith;

they mean you are living in truth. The human soul was not made for death. We were created in the image of the eternal God. Something inside us knows instinctively that death is an interruption, a fracture in the harmony for which we were made. Augustine said, "You have made us for Yourself, O Lord, and our hearts are restless until they rest in You." That restlessness is not anxiety. It is the soul remembering Eden and longing for home.

If the fear of death shakes us, it is because we sense how precious life is. You have lived, loved, chosen, hoped; you have become someone in the eyes of God. When illness threatens the body, it can feel as though the very self is under threat. But this fear is answered not by ignoring mortality, nor by pretending death is natural or serene, but by turning to the One who entered death and transformed it from within. Christian hope does not begin by denying death exists. It begins by declaring that death is no longer master.

The first truth you must hold close is this: your identity is beyond the reach of death. Not even for a moment does God see you as reducible to your illness, or to the frailty of your body, or to the statistics of your condition. You are not simply a biological organism fighting disease; you are a person — a soul — a being fashioned in the image of God, known and loved from before the foundation of the world. "Before I formed you in the womb, I knew you" (Jeremiah 1:5). That knowledge is not medical; it is covenantal. God does not know you the way doctors know charts. God knows you the way a father knows a child, the way a lover knows the beloved, the way the Creator knows the masterpiece fashioned by His own hands.

Your soul is not fragile. It is not at the mercy of illness. Gregory of Nyssa wrote that the soul's capacity for God makes it "larger than the universe," because the universe is finite but the soul can receive the Infinite. Illness can touch the surface of your life, but not the depths. It can weaken your limbs but cannot shake the truth of who you are.

You are the one God calls by name: "You are Mine" (Isaiah 43:1). A body may falter; a soul held in God does not.

Cancer can alter appearance, energy, mobility — but it cannot erase identity. Identity rooted in God is not something that decays. It is not written in the lines of your face or in the strength of your muscles. Identity is the eternal truth spoken by God over your life: "I have created you for my glory" (Isaiah 43:7). John Paul II wrote that the dignity of the person is "indestructible," because it is grounded in the divine image and sustained by divine love. Nothing in the realm of biology can diminish a reality grounded in the life of God.

When the body grows weaker, it is easy to confuse physical decline with personal diminishment. But Scripture teaches the opposite. St. Paul, who knew suffering intimately, wrote, "Though our outer self is wasting away, our inner self is being renewed day by day" (2 Corinthians 4:16). This is not poetic optimism. It is theological truth. As the outer life grows fragile, the inner life often grows fierce, luminous, purified, simplified. Suffering has a way of distilling what truly matters, revealing the heart's deepest loves, awakening a longing for God that daily life can too easily numb. What the world calls loss, heaven often calls transformation.

And here is a truth Christ Himself speaks with gentle authority: cancer cannot touch the soul. It can afflict flesh, weaken the immune system, send waves of fatigue through your days — but it cannot reach the sanctuary where God dwells within you. Jesus says, "Do not fear those who kill the body but cannot kill the soul" (Matthew 10:28). He is speaking tenderly: illness may strike the body, but the soul remains untouched, held, guarded. The real you — your mind, your memories, your love, your will, your relationship with God — rests in a place unreachable by disease.

St. Irenaeus famously wrote, "The glory of God is man fully alive." He did not mean physically vigorous; he meant alive in God. A person undergoing treatment, bedridden, exhausted, still radiates the glory of God because the glory is not in bodily strength but in the soul's capacity to love, to trust, to endure, to cling to God even in weakness. Your soul remains intact, luminous, precious. The illness cannot rewrite the story God has written over your life.

And this leads to a deeper truth still: the Father holds every moment that frightens you. Nothing you fear is unknown to Him. Nothing surprises Him. Not a single moment of anxiety passes unnoticed. Jesus assures us that even the smallest creatures are under the Father's watch: "Not a sparrow falls to the ground without your Father's knowledge... Fear not, you are of more value than many sparrows" (Matthew 10:29–31). If God's providence extends to the fall of a sparrow, how much more does it extend to the trembling of your heart?

Psalm 139 describes a God who knows us so deeply that even our sighs become prayer. "You discern my thoughts from afar... even before a word is on my tongue, You know it completely." When fear rises in you, God is already there. When you imagine the future and feel a knot in your chest, God is already present in that future moment, waiting to meet you with grace you cannot yet see. There is no territory — emotional, physical, spiritual — where God is absent. "If I make my bed in Sheol, You are there" (Psalm 139:8). David does not mean metaphorically. He means literally: even in death, God is present.

There is a moment in the Gospels that reveals this truth with startling tenderness. A woman suffering for twelve years fought her way through a crowd simply to touch the fringe of Jesus' garment. Her illness had driven her into isolation, but it had not hidden her from God. When she touched Him, Jesus stopped, searched the crowd, and said, "Who touched me?" (Mark 5:30). He knew the answer, of course. He asked so she would know she had been seen. God is never indifferent to hidden suffering. He is attentive to every moment your heart tightens, every night fear wakes you, every time you wonder how much more your body can bear. The Father is not far away; He is closer than your own breath.

Even at the threshold of death, God's gaze remains tender. The thief on the cross turned to Jesus with nothing left — no life to offer, no reputation, no accomplishments, not even the strength to kneel. He had only the frail request of a dying man: "Remember me." And Jesus answered immediately and intimately: "Today you will be with Me in paradise" (Luke 23:42–43). Death did not frighten Jesus. He stepped into it willingly. And because He stepped into it, He transformed it. Death, which had always been a place of fear, became a place where the voice of Christ can be heard.

This is why you can face mortality with confidence: Christ has entered death so you will never face it alone. No human being has ever stood before death without trembling — except the One who walked into death to conquer it. Hebrews says that by dying, Christ "destroyed the one who had the power of death, that is, the devil," and freed all who lived in fear of it (Hebrews 2:14–15). Imagine that: death itself dismantled from the inside. The great enemy broken open. A prison turned into a doorway.

Hans Urs von Balthasar once said that Christ descended into death so fully that "there is no night into which He has not gone ahead of us." That means there is no moment in your future — not even the moment of death — where Christ will not already be present. You will never arrive at a place where Jesus is not waiting. This is not sentiment; it is the very heart of Christian revelation. Christ has filled death with His presence. What once was empty is now occupied by God. What once was final is now a passage. What once was enemy is now servant to glory.

On Holy Saturday — the day Christ lay in the tomb — the world saw silence. Stillness. But the early Church knew that this stillness was not inactivity; it was divine work at its deepest. An ancient homily for Holy Saturday imagines Christ entering the realm of the dead like a warrior entering a battlefield, seeking Adam, calling out, "Awake, O sleeper, rise from the dead, for I am the life of the dead." The point is clear: death is no longer the place where life ends. It is the place where Christ begins His greatest work.

And so, when illness forces you to look toward the horizon of mortality, you do not look alone. You do not look into darkness. You look into a place where Christ is already standing. He is not at the far end calling you from a distance; He is beside you, walking with you, guiding your steps toward a future where His victory will become your own. Fear may rise, but that fear is not the whole truth. The whole truth is this: you belong to the One who has conquered death.

The promises of Jesus were not poetic metaphors. "I go to prepare a place for you... I will come again and take you to Myself" (John 14:2–3). These are the words of a Bridegroom speaking to His beloved. He is not promising a distant kingdom. He is promising His presence. Heaven is not primarily a place; it is a relationship brought to perfect fulfillment. Death does not end your story; it completes it. What begins in faith ends in vision. What begins in yearning ends in union.

For the one who suffers illness, it may feel as though death casts a shadow over everything. But shadows only exist when a greater light is shining behind them. The Resurrection reveals that the greater light is Christ Himself, the Lamb whose life cannot be extinguished. "I am the Living One," He tells John. "Behold, I died, and I am alive forevermore, and I hold the keys of death and Hades" (Revelation 1:18). If Christ holds the keys, then death holds no one captive. Not even you.

As your body weakens, your soul does not weaken. It is refined. Strengthened. Clarified. The saints consistently testify that grace often burns brightest in those whose bodies are failing. St. Thérèse, who died of tuberculosis at twenty-four, said that suffering purified her vision until she saw God everywhere. John Paul II, in his final illness, became a living icon of redemptive vulnerability. When the body's strength wanes, the soul's reliance on God intensifies. Death cannot touch this. It cannot extinguish prayer. It cannot silence love. It cannot erase the grace growing in you with every surrendered fear, every whispered prayer, every day you choose to trust even when trust feels fragile.

The world measures decline by what the body loses. Heaven measures growth by what the soul receives. Illness may narrow your physical abilities, but in ways unseen, it can widen your capacity for God. Mortality becomes not a threat to identity but a doorway through which identity is fulfilled. You are not losing yourself — you are drawing closer to the One who has held you from the beginning.

If there is one truth suffering makes clearer than any other, it is that love endures. Every moment you have given in love, every sacrifice you have made, every act of kindness, every prayer whispered on behalf of others—these are untouched by illness and untouched by death. Paul writes that "love never ends" (1 Corinthians 13:8). Not love in general. *Your* love. The love you have given and the love you have received are eternal realities, stored in the heart of God. Death cannot undo them. Cancer cannot diminish them. Memory may fade, the body may weaken, but love is rooted in eternity. What is done in love is done forever.

This is why Christians speak of death not as annihilation but as homecoming. The Father who formed you in love and sustained you in love now waits to receive you in love. Jesus does not hand you off to an unknown destiny; He brings you to the Father with His own pierced hands. The Gospel is not the story of a God who simply forgives sins; it is the story of a God who refuses to lose His children. The entire Bible can be read as God's relentless determination to bring His people home. Illness may hasten your awareness of this truth, but it does not change the truth itself: you are wanted, you are awaited, and you will be welcomed.

When the moment of death finally comes, it will not be an instant of abandonment but an instant of union. St. Francis of Assisi called death "Sister Death"—not because it is gentle in itself, but because Christ has made it gentle for the believer. He has transformed it from punishment into passage, from terror into embrace. When your eyes close to this world, they do not open into darkness; they open into God. When your hands can no longer hold the people you love, the hands of Christ will hold you. When your breath leaves your body, it rises into the breath of the Spirit who gave you life.

Nothing in your future is unknown to God. Nothing lies outside His providence. Not even the timing or manner of your death. Psalm 31 says, "My times are in Your hands," a truth that becomes luminous when suffering makes you aware of how little control you possess. You are not drifting toward an unmarked horizon. You are being led. Guided. Accompanied. The Shepherd who walked with you through every valley of this life will walk with you through the final valley as well. "Even though I walk through the valley of the shadow of death, I will fear no evil, for You are with me" (Psalm 23:4). The psalmist does not hope God will be with him; he declares it as fact. God does not leave His sheep in their hour of need. He draws even closer.

And this confidence does not belong only to the saints; it belongs to you. You may feel weak. You may feel frightened. You may feel unprepared. But Christ does not ask for strength you do not have. He asks only for trust—not perfect trust, not unshakable trust, just the small, sincere trust of a child resting in a father's arms. Trust is not the absence of fear; trust is letting God hold your fear. Trust is not certainty about outcomes; trust is certainty about God's heart.

Your suffering does not mean God has abandoned you. It means you are walking a path Christ Himself walked first. It means the Father is drawing you nearer. It means heaven is closer than you think. Your life is not sliding toward oblivion. It is moving toward fulfillment. Every day you endure in faith, even if your faith feels thin, is a step toward glory.

And when that glory comes, every fear you carry now will dissolve in the light of God's face. The questions you whisper in the dark will be answered not with sentences but with embrace. The sorrow you feel will be lifted, gathered, transformed. The wounds you bear—emotional, spiritual, physical—will shine like Christ's own wounds, radiant with the story of how God carried you.

This is what death cannot touch:
your identity as God's child,
your soul shaped in His image,
your story held in His hands,
your destiny anchored in His love.

Even now, as you read these words, He is closer than your breath. Closer than your fears. Closer than the illness in your body. The God who overcame death does not let His children walk into the unknown alone. When you take your final step in this life, you will step into the arms that have been waiting for you since the beginning.

Death cannot change who you are.
Death cannot silence the love God has for you.
Death cannot break the promise Christ has made.
Death cannot touch the soul that rests in the Father's hands.
You are held.
You are safe.
You belong to the God who lives forever,
and because He lives, you too shall live.

Twenty-Two

Healing: In This Life and the Next

Every person who suffers longs for healing. It rises from the heart as naturally as breath, a desire woven into our very being by the God who made us. When illness enters a life, the desire for healing does not need to be taught or justified. It awakens immediately, instinctively: the longing to be restored, to be made whole, to return to the life that once existed before hospitals and waiting rooms and treatment plans shaped the rhythm of each day. This longing is not a sign of weak faith. It is not a denial of God's will. It is one of the most profoundly human desires we possess, because it reflects the original design of our Creator. We were made for life, for wholeness, for communion. Something deep in the soul knows that suffering is foreign to the world as God intended it. Our longing for healing is our soul remembering paradise.

Throughout the Gospels, Jesus receives this longing with tenderness. People approached Him with desperation and simplicity, crying out, "Lord, that I may see," "Master, heal my servant," "If You will, You can make me clean." Not once did Jesus accuse them of self-focus or impatience. He never told a suffering person that their desire for healing was misguided. He met their request with compassion. He touched the eyes of the blind, He raised the paralytic from his mat, He restored the outcast to his community. Every physical healing in Scripture is a revelation of God's heart: a heart that delights in mending what is broken, restoring what is lost, lifting what is crushed. The desire for healing is not something God asks you to suppress; it is something He asks you to bring to Him.

But the longing for healing often carries fears alongside it—fears we speak only in whispers. What if healing does not come? What if prayers seem unanswered? What if the body continues to weaken despite the pleading of the soul? These are not questions of rebellion. They are questions born of love for life, for family, for the future. And God does not turn away from these questions. He listens. He understands. The God who formed your body knows the ache of illness from the inside, because Christ carried it in His own flesh. Nothing you feel is foreign to Him.

Yet healing in Scripture—and healing in the Christian life—is far deeper than the restoration of physical strength. Physical healing matters, and we must never downplay its importance. When Jesus healed bodies, He revealed the nearness of the Kingdom. But every healing in the Gospels had one thing in common: it was temporary. Eyes that regained sight would one day close in death. Limbs that were strengthened would again weaken with age. Bodies restored would one day be placed in the earth. Healing now is precious, but it is not the fullness. It is a signpost pointing to something eternal.

Still, God does heal physically in this life. Sometimes He heals in ways so clear and unmistakable that the only possible explanation is His mercy. The Gospels overflow with such moments, and the Church's history continues to testify to them—through the saints, through the sacraments, through places like Lourdes where the sick go with hope not in physicians but in Christ. When God grants physical healing, it is a gift of compassion. It is a glimpse of the Kingdom where sickness will cease forever. But when He does not, it is not a sign of abandonment. It is not a failure of prayer. It is not the measure of your worth or faith.

A prayer unanswered in the way we hoped is not a prayer unheard. God treasures every prayer as incense rising before His throne, Revelation tells us. He absorbs them into His heart. He answers them, though not always according to the script we imagine. Sometimes the healing comes quickly, like the blind man who suddenly saw light. Sometimes it comes slowly, in the unfolding of courage, hope, and trust within the soul. Sometimes the healing the heart longs for is given only in eternity, where the limits and sufferings of this life fall away. But all prayer is answered.

For many who suffer, the deepest and most surprising form of healing does not begin in the body but in the soul. Illness often exposes places within us we never knew needed attention: old wounds, hidden fears, attachments that weighed us down without our noticing. As physical strength wanes, spiritual sensitivity often sharpens. Pride softens. Compassion deepens. Gratitude grows. Love purifies. The saints describe this not as psychological coping but as sanctification—the soul being shaped into the likeness of Christ.

St. Paul's thorn in the flesh is a profound example. He begged God for relief, not once but repeatedly. And God did not remove it. Instead He said, "My grace is sufficient for you, for My power is made perfect in weakness" (2 Corinthians 12:9). Paul discovered that God sometimes heals not by removing the affliction but by transforming the one who suffers. Interior healing does not eliminate the wound; it fills it with God's presence. It does not undo the cross; it reveals resurrection power within it.

This interior healing is not smaller than physical healing. In many ways, it is greater. A restored body is a blessing for the years of this life. A restored soul is a blessing for eternity. Illness can clarify what truly matters: love, forgiveness, trust, surrender. It can draw a person toward God in ways comfort never could. It can teach the heart to pray with deeper honesty, to depend more freely, to let go of burdens long carried. Many of the most radiant saints—Job, Tobit, Thérèse, John Paul II—became luminous precisely through the suffering that afflicted their bodies. Illness did not diminish their holiness; it deepened it.

Yet interior healing, as beautiful as it is, is not the final healing God promises. The deepest promise of Christianity is not escape from suffering but transformation of suffering, and beyond transformation, resurrection. The Creed proclaims the resurrection of the body not as a metaphor but as the destiny of every believer. What is sown perishable will be raised imperishable, Paul says. What is sown in weakness will be raised in power. The body that now grows tired, that now battles illness, that now bears scars—this body will rise. Not replaced. Not discarded. Raised.

This promise is not poetry. It is the Christian hope anchored in the risen Christ. When the disciples saw Jesus after the Resurrection, they did not see a ghost or a vapor. They saw a body. A body that could be touched. A body that ate with them. A body marked by wounds—wounds that had become radiant. These wounds were not erased. They were transfigured. They no longer spoke of violence or fear; they spoke of love carried to its completion. In keeping His wounds, Christ was teaching us something essential: nothing offered to God in love is lost. Nothing given, nothing endured, nothing surrendered is wasted. Even the most painful parts of our story can shine with glory in His presence.

Your body may now feel fragile, and perhaps it frightens you. You may notice losses you never imagined—strength, mobility, energy, appetite, familiar rhythms of life. But these losses do not define you, and they do not dictate your future. In Christ, the broken becomes the doorway to the unbreakable. The wounded becomes the place where divine light enters. The sick body of today is not the body you will carry forever. Death is not the final word; transformation is. This is the meaning of the Resurrection: the last word belongs to God, not to cancer.

Still, the journey toward that final healing is not easy. There are days when prayer feels heavy and God feels distant. There are days when the doctor's report shakes the heart more than any Scripture verse seems to steady it. There are days filled with quiet fears you cannot fully express even to the people who love you most. These experiences do not make you weak in faith. They make you human. Even Jesus cried out in anguish in Gethsemane and breathed His last in darkness on the Cross. He knows this path from the inside. He walks it with you, not as an observer but as a companion.

One of the greatest mysteries of suffering is the way God weaves together healing and holiness. Sometimes He restores the body and strengthens faith through the miracle. Sometimes He allows the illness to remain and strengthens faith through the endurance. In both cases, His purpose is love. In both cases, His presence is near. In both cases, He gathers fruit from the offering you make, fruit often unseen by you in this life. The saints often wrote that the hidden moments of trust offered in suffering are among the most powerful prayers a soul can give. Not because God delights in pain—He does not—but because trust given freely in the midst of pain is trust purified of all lesser motives.

There is another dimension of healing that illness often awakens: reconciliation. Illness can bring back into focus relationships that have drifted, words left unsaid, forgiveness withheld too long. It can prompt the soul to forgive, to release old griefs, to speak love more freely, to embrace more gently. These movements of the heart are not small healings. They are profound healings—the kind Christ spoke of when He said He came to bind up the broken-hearted. Sometimes the deepest wounds are not in the body but in memories, regrets, family histories, unresolved tensions. Illness can become the sacred hour when God moves quietly through the corridors of the soul, closing old wounds and making space for new peace.

And yet even these beautiful healings, which matter so deeply, are not the final promise. The final healing is the vision of God "face to face" that Scripture says surpasses all understanding. The Book of Revelation describes it with breathtaking simplicity: "He will wipe every tear from their eyes, and death shall be no more" (Revelation 21:4). Not one tear forgotten. Not one ache ignored. Not one fear unnoticed. God gathers them all into His eternal embrace and transforms them into joy. What is healed partially here will be healed perfectly there. What is begun now will be completed in glory.

The Christian does not hope vaguely for "a better place." The Christian hopes for a new creation. A restored world. A resurrected body. A communion of saints. A joy that cannot be shaken. A love that cannot be lost. A life that cannot end. Cancer cannot touch this future. No disease can diminish it. No diagnosis can shorten it. Your destiny is not frailty. It is glory.

Yet while we wait for that day, there is comfort God gives in the present that is not merely spiritual but deeply human: the comfort of being held, accompanied, known. Christ does not promise that suffering will vanish, but He promises that you will never suffer alone. He promises that no prayer will ever fall into an empty space. He promises that He is working—silently, mysteriously, powerfully—through every moment of faith you offer. Whether your body is restored now or in the Resurrection, the Love that holds you is the same.

There is a tenderness in the way God remains present in suffering that cannot be easily described but is unmistakably real. Sometimes it appears in the strength to do something simple—sit up, speak gently, endure another treatment. Sometimes it appears in the peace that slips unexpectedly into the room during prayer. Sometimes it reveals itself in the way a loved one leans close, sensing your need without you having to say a word. These small moments are sacraments of God's nearness. They are not accidental. They are signs that the Shepherd walks with His sheep through the valley, guiding not with explanations but with presence.

Healing also takes the form of courage—courage you may not even recognize as courage. Courage is not the absence of fear. Courage is moving forward in love despite the fear. When you step into the clinic knowing the day will be difficult, that is courage. When you choose to hope even though outcomes remain uncertain, that is courage. When you speak gently to someone even as your own heart trembles, that is courage. When you pray without feeling anything, simply because you trust God deserves your prayer, that is courage. These acts, small as they may seem, are heroic in the eyes of the One who sees in secret.

The Church teaches that suffering united to Christ becomes a participation in His redeeming work. This is not a poetic notion but a theological truth rooted in Colossians 1:24, where St. Paul says, "I rejoice in my sufferings for your sake, and in my flesh I complete what is lacking in Christ's afflictions for the sake of His Body, the Church." Nothing is lacking in Christ's sacrifice except our willingness to join our lives to His. When you offer your suffering—not merely endure it, but offer it—it becomes mysteriously fruitful. You may never see the fruit in this life, but God gathers it nonetheless. A whispered prayer in a hospital bed may strengthen a soul on the other side of the world. A quiet act of trust at dawn may touch a heart years later in ways only God can orchestrate.

This is one of the most beautiful and hidden healings God performs: He transforms suffering into love. He does not merely help us endure it;

He invites us to enter it with Him so that our wounds become conduits of grace. Christ's own resurrected body still bore the marks of the nails—not because they were signs of defeat, but because they had become signs of love. In the same way, the wounds we carry, physical or emotional, can become in Christ the places where His grace shines most clearly.

There is also a healing that comes through the sacraments, which are not symbolic gestures but the real channels of divine life. The Anointing of the Sick is not a ritual reserved for the final moments of life. It is a sacrament of strength, offered by Christ Himself through the priest. It brings forgiveness, peace, and often a deep sense of God's presence. Countless people testify that after receiving it, even if the body remains fragile, something in the soul settles into trust. The Eucharist, too, becomes a kind of healing—Christ feeding you with His own life, strengthening you from within. Confession brings healing of conscience, lifting burdens long carried. Each sacrament is a reminder that healing is not something we must extract from God; it is something God freely pours into us.

But the deepest healing God promises cannot be fully seen until the moment when this life gives way to the next. Death is often imagined as an ending, a severing, a rupture. Scripture views it differently. For the Christian, death is the final healing of all that remains wounded. It is the doorway Christ Himself passed through, transfiguring it from a prison into a passageway. "For to me, to live is Christ and to die is gain," Paul writes—not because life is unimportant, but because death ushers us into the presence of the One we have loved through faith. Death is not the shattering of identity; it is the unveiling of identity. It is not the end of the story; it is the chapter in which everything broken is made whole.

When that moment comes—whether soon or far from now—you will not face it alone. The Father who created you, the Son who redeemed you, and the Spirit who has lived in you will be nearer than your breath. The Church will pray for you. The saints will surround you. The angels will accompany you. And the One who bore wounds for your sake will stand before you, His love stronger than every fear. "I go to prepare a place for you," He said. That promise has no expiration.

The hope of eternal healing does not diminish the value of this life; it illuminates it. Knowing that God will make all things new gives us the freedom to live this moment fully—tenderly, gratefully, courageously. It means every prayer matters. Every tear matters. Every act of love, however small, becomes a thread God weaves into the tapestry of eternity. Nothing offered to Him disappears into silence. Nothing poured out in faith returns empty. Your journey—its joys, its wounds, its prayers, its waiting—has a place in the story of salvation far greater than you can now imagine.

You may wonder whether your suffering has changed you—whether it has stripped away joys you once knew or capacities you once possessed. Yet even as illness narrows some parts of life, it often expands others. It stretches the heart. It softens it in ways comfort never could. It teaches you how to cherish moments that once slipped past unnoticed: the warmth of a hand, the sound of a familiar voice, the quiet peace of a morning when pain lifts for a while. These are not small things. They are glimpses of the world God is preparing for you, where joy will not be fleeting but complete.

And when the body falters, when strength fades, when you feel the limits of what you can endure, remember this: God's healing does not depend on your resilience. It depends on His love. You do not need to be brave every moment. You do not need to carry a hero's composure. You do not need to approach God with eloquence. Healing begins not with strength but with surrender. Not with flawless faith but with willingness: "Lord, be with me." That simple prayer opens the soul to the mercy that has been pursuing you since the day you were born.

There are forms of healing, too, that reveal themselves only to those who suffer. A person undergoing illness often becomes a beacon to others without realizing it. Loved ones watching from the outside witness courage that inspires their own. They learn patience from your patience, tenderness from your vulnerability, compassion from your endurance. Your suffering becomes a school of love for them. You might not feel strong, but they see strength. You might feel fear, but they see faith. God uses your journey to touch lives in ways hidden even from you. This is not romanticising suffering. It is recognising the quiet ministry God brings forth through those who suffer with Him.

The final healing promised by God does not negate the longing for healing now. It completes it. It affirms that your desire to be restored is not an illusion but an echo of the destiny God has prepared for you. The body you now inhabit with its frailties and limits will one day be raised in glory. The love you have shared will not be lost. The prayers you have prayed will not be forgotten. The tears you have shed will not remain unhealed. Christ keeps His wounds because He has made a promise about yours: they will shine.

And so, in this life, pray boldly for healing. Pray honestly, pray freely, pray without embarrassment. Christ delights in these prayers. Pray with expectation, knowing He hears. But also pray with trust, knowing that His way of healing may go deeper than the body, may take longer than you hoped, may unfold in ways you cannot yet see. His timing is perfect even when hidden. His mercy is at work even when silent. His love is accomplishing more than your heart can now perceive.

When the final day comes—the day God has chosen not as a punishment but as a homecoming—you will discover that healing was never withheld. It was being prepared. In that moment, every fear will evaporate. Every wound will be soothed. Every tear will be wiped away by the hand of God Himself. You will see Him face to face, and in His gaze you will recognise the purpose behind every moment of your journey. The silence, the prayers, the nights of fear, the fragile faith—they will all open into joy.

Until that day, Christ walks with you. He remains the Healer, whether He restores the body or strengthens the soul, whether He grants recovery now or prepares you for glory later. In His hands, no suffering is wasted, no prayer is lost, and no life ends in defeat. Healing is already taking root in ways beyond your sight, and the fullness of that healing waits for you in the Kingdom prepared from the foundation of the world.

Your story does not end with illness. It does not end with decline. It does not end with death. Your story ends in God—who makes all things new, who lifts you into everlasting life, and who has already begun the healing that will one day be complete.

Epilogue

Everything you have read in these pages has been an attempt to place words around a mystery far greater than any book can capture: the mystery of a God who stays. A God who enters the sorrow we cannot avoid, who walks the roads we never would have chosen, who listens to questions we never wanted to ask. You have travelled through valleys of fear and nights of silence, moments when the body faltered, moments when the heart trembled, moments when hope felt fragile. Yet through every page, through every chapter, a single truth waited quietly beneath the surface, like a refrain written into the soul of the world: you have never been alone.

If this book has revealed anything, it is the shape of God's nearness. Not a nearness reserved only for the strong or the serene, but a nearness that bends toward the weary, the frightened, the sick, the uncertain. The God of Scripture is not distant from suffering; He steps into it. He weeps at the tomb of a friend. He sweats blood in Gethsemane. He hangs upon a Cross not as an observer but as a companion, entering the depths of the human condition so that no valley would ever remain Godless again. If you have ever wondered where He is in your suffering, the answer is simple and staggering: He is where He has always been—beside His children, carrying what they cannot carry.

And in the long nights of illness, when the world grows small and the hours wait heavy on your chest, when all you can offer is a whisper or a sigh, He receives it with the tenderness of one who understands. Prayer does not need eloquence to reach Him; it needs honesty. He receives the broken prayer, the wordless prayer, the tired prayer. In weakness, prayer becomes truer, because it rises from the core of who you are. Not the self you present when life is easy, but the self that stands before God without strength to spare. That self is precious to Him.

You have learned along the way that suffering does not erase dignity. It does not diminish the image of God in you, nor does it weaken your place in His heart. Illness may change how you move, how you feel, how you navigate each day, but it cannot change who you are. You are the one God loves. You are the one Christ died for. You are the one the Spirit strengthens in secret moments you cannot yet see. The world measures life by health, productivity, accomplishments. God measures life by love. And love is often purer when all else falls away.

You have also seen that suffering, when lived with even a small spark of faith, becomes strangely luminous. People around you are changed, not because you perform acts of heroism, but because courage is revealed in endurance, compassion deepens in vulnerability, and faith shines most clearly when the path is darkest. What you have endured has not been wasted. God has woven it quietly into the stories of others in ways you may never fully know on this side of eternity. Your journey has not been a private one; it has been a ministry—hidden, humble, holy.

And now, as these final pages draw near, the temptation might arise to wonder whether the comfort of these reflections will fade when the book closes, whether the strength you felt while reading will slip away when tomorrow brings its demands. But the grace sustaining you was never the grace of a book. It was the grace of a Person. Christ does not disappear when the last sentence ends. He does not retreat

Epilogue

when the cover shuts. The One who spoke the universe into being is the same One who walks with you to every appointment, sits beside you in every waiting room, stands near your bed in the quiet hours of the night. His companionship does not weaken with time; it deepens.

He knows the things you have not spoken aloud—the fears you carry silently to spare those you love, the hopes you hesitate to voice because they seem too fragile, the memories that rise unbidden when the room grows still. He knows the burden of wanting to protect your family from worry even while you yourself feel small and unsteady. He knows the ache behind the simple desire for one more good day, one more moment of clarity, one more breath of peace. Nothing hidden from Him is ignored by Him.

And because He knows, He carries you. Not metaphorically. Not symbolically. Truly. The strength you have found on days you expected to collapse did not come only from within you—it was lent to you by the One who promised, "I am with you always." The peace that settled over your heart at unexpected moments was not your imagination—it was His hand resting upon you. The courage that rose in you when you feared the next step was not self-manufactured—it was His Spirit breathing within your spirit, reminding you that you are never left to face anything alone.

Even now, as you reach the end of this book, Christ holds the future you fear. He goes ahead of you into every unknown. He stands already in tomorrow's appointments, tomorrow's scans, tomorrow's conversations, tomorrow's tears. Nothing that awaits you in the coming hours or days or years will ever meet you for the first time; it will always meet Him first. He is the God who walks ahead of His people, who prepares the road even when the road is hard. Your life is not drifting toward uncertainty. It is being guided, moment by moment, into the heart of God.

And the nights that still unsettle you—the nights when sleep refuses to come, when thoughts grow loud, when silence feels heavy—those nights are not abandoned spaces. They are the hours in which Christ keeps vigil beside you. "He who keeps Israel neither slumbers nor sleeps." When you lie awake with trembling thoughts, He is awake with you. When you feel the weight of the dark settling in your room, He fills that space with His quiet presence. The night belongs not to fear, but to the God who created it, the God who watches over His beloved while they rest or weep or wait for dawn. You are held even then.

If you worry about your family—about the burden your illness places on those you love—Christ sees that too. He knows the sorrow you feel when you watch their concern, the tenderness that aches because you wish you could shield them from all of this. But the love they give you is not a burden; it is their vocation, their holiness, their participation in the mystery of grace. You are not taking from them. You are giving them a place to practice love in its purest form. And God is forming their hearts even as He is forming yours. What you share in these days is sacred.

And if there are moments when you feel weak or dependent or embarrassed by the help you need, remember that Christ Himself allowed Simon to carry His Cross. The Son of God was not ashamed to lean on another. He did not resist the hands that lifted His burden. He let love assist Him, not because He lacked divinity, but because He embraced humanity. When you let others help you, you do not diminish your dignity; you imitate your Savior.

So let this be the word that stands above every chapter you have read: you are held. Not for a moment, not occasionally, not only when your faith feels strong—you are held always. Held when your body trembles, held when your prayers are small, held when your heart aches, held when fear rises, held when peace returns, held when the path forward is unclear, held when hope brightens, held when strength fades. The

Epilogue

hands that hold you are the hands that shaped the stars, the hands that touched the sick, the hands that were pierced out of love for you. Those hands will never let you go.

And now, as this book comes to its final page, let your heart receive not an ending but a blessing. Let these words rest upon you the way a gentle hand rests upon a weary shoulder:

May Christ walk with you into every room you enter.

May His peace guard your mind when fear rises.

May His tenderness meet you in the places you feel most fragile.

May His strength steady you when the road feels steep.

May His wounds remind you that your wounds are seen, honoured, and never carried alone.

May His Resurrection keep your hope from fading.

May His Spirit breathe within you when your own breath feels thin.

May His Father be your refuge, your shelter, your comfort, your home.

And in the hours when you cannot pray, may the prayers of the Church—on earth and in heaven—surround you like a great cloud of witnesses, lifting you before God with love that does not tire. May the angels keep watch at your bedside. May the saints hold vigil for you. May Mary, the Mother who stood beneath the Cross, stand beside you with her quiet, fearless faith.

Above all, may you know deep in your soul what this entire journey has been whispering from the beginning:

you are not alone.

Not in suffering.

Not in waiting.

Not in treatment.

Not in fear.

Not in the long nights.

Not in the uncertain days.

Not in the thoughts you do not speak aloud.
Not in the questions that linger.
Not in the hopes you still carry.
Not in the moments when courage falters.
Not in the moments when peace returns.
Christ is with you.
Christ is for you.
Christ is nearer to you than your own breath.

So let the final word of this book become the first word of the days ahead—

a word you can return to again and again, a word stronger than cancer, stronger than fear, stronger than the darkest night, stronger even than death itself:

You are held.

APPENDIX A — PRAYERS FOR STRENGTH

Breath Prayers

1. Jesus, stay with me—my heart needs Your nearness more than my strength.
2. Lord, be my peace when fear rises and my courage feels small.
3. Father, hold me close; I cannot walk today without Your hand.
4. Spirit of God, breathe in me what I no longer have the energy to give.
5. Jesus, carry what I cannot carry—let Your mercy be enough for this moment.

Prayers in the Hospital Room

1. Lord, You who walked into the rooms of the sick with tenderness, walk with me now into this place of uncertainty. Let Your presence quiet my fear and fill this room with the peace only You can give.
2. Christ, as I wait for doctors and nurses, steady my heart. Bless

those who care for me with wisdom and gentleness, and let every touch, word, and decision be guided by Your compassion.
3. Jesus, when the machines hum and the hours stretch long, sit beside me the way You sat with the suffering. Let this room become a sanctuary where Your love meets my weakness.
4. Lord, if difficult news comes, let Your voice be louder than my fear. Wrap me in the same courage You gave to the saints who trusted You through every valley.
5. Father, in this hospital bed I feel small, but Your love fills the whole of my life. Be my refuge now. Let Your peace settle over me like a soft blanket, guarding my heart through every moment of this day.

Prayers for the Night

1. Jesus, as darkness settles and sleep feels far away, stay awake with me. Let Your presence become the light that quiets my thoughts and comforts my heart.
2. Lord, when fear whispers loudly in the night, speak Your word of peace: "Do not be afraid, for I am with you." Let that promise rest upon me like a shield.
3. Father, when my mind will not quiet and memories or fears overwhelm me, place Your hand upon my soul and calm the storm within.
4. Christ, You prayed in Gethsemane through the long and sorrowful night. Stay with me in my night, and let me find rest in the nearness of Your suffering love.
5. God of Israel, You neither slumber nor sleep. Keep watch over me now. Guard my breathing, my thoughts, my heart, and let Your peace be my pillow until morning comes.

APPENDIX A — PRAYERS FOR STRENGTH

Prayers Before Treatment

1. Lord Jesus, as I enter this treatment, walk before me. Strengthen my mind, steady my nerves, and guide every hand that cares for me. Let this be a moment where grace is at work in ways I cannot yet see.
2. Father, I place my body and soul into Your keeping. Bless the medicine, bless the process, bless the journey ahead. Let Your healing love surround me as I take this step.
3. Holy Spirit, quiet my fears and fill me with courage. Give me the grace to trust that I am not facing this alone, for You are my helper and my strength.
4. Christ, who touched the sick with compassion, lay Your hand upon me now. Let this treatment become an instrument of Your care, and give me the patience to endure what is difficult.
5. Lord, as I wait for the procedure to begin, hold my heart in peace. I do not know what today will bring, but I know You will be in every moment of it. Let that be enough for me.

Prayers for Fear

1. Jesus, when fear rises like a tide within me, speak again the words You spoke on the stormy sea: "Take heart; it is I. Do not be afraid." Let Your voice steady what trembles in me.
2. Lord, I confess my fear to You—not as a failure, but as a child turning to a Father. Hold my heart in Your hands and teach me to breathe in Your peace.
3. Christ, You knelt in Gethsemane with a heart full of sorrow; stay near me when fear presses heavily on my chest. Let me lean into Your courage when I cannot find my own.

4. Father, when fear imagines the worst, help me remember that You are already in every tomorrow I dread. Nothing awaits me that has not first passed through Your love.
5. Holy Spirit, fill the spaces where my anxiety lives. Let Your calm settle over my mind like gentle rain, softening everything that feels hard and overwhelming.

Prayers for Loved Ones

1. Father, bless the ones who walk this journey with me. Strengthen their hearts, protect their peace, and let them feel Your presence as deeply as I do in this moment.
2. Lord Jesus, I place my family in Your hands. Carry what they cannot speak aloud, comfort what they cannot explain, and let our home become a place where Your love is felt in every room.
3. Holy Spirit, give courage to those who care for me—spouses, children, siblings, friends. Fill them with patience, tenderness, and hope. Let their love become a reflection of Yours.
4. Christ, when my illness weighs on the hearts of those I love, lift their burdens. Whisper to them that none of this is wasted, and that their presence strengthens me more than they know.
5. Heavenly Father, shelter the ones who worry over me. Give them rest when they are tired, joy when the days feel long, and confidence that You are working in ways they cannot yet see.

Prayers When You Cannot Pray

1. Lord, I cannot pray tonight—my heart is tired, my mind is numb. So let my silence be my prayer, and let Your mercy fill what I

cannot offer.
2. Jesus, I feel nothing right now. Hold me anyway. Receive my emptiness as the only prayer I can give, and make it enough.
3. Spirit of God, pray within me when I have no words. Let Your sighs, deeper than speech, rise before the Father in my place.
4. Christ, gather my weakness into Your own. When my faith feels small and my courage disappears, let Your faithfulness carry me.
5. Father, I rest in You without words, without clarity, without strength—only trust. You know my heart better than I do. Let that be my prayer today.

APPENDIX B — SCRIPTURES FOR THE DARK HOURS

WHEN FEAR RISES

For the moments when fear grows louder than peace.

Isaiah 41:10 (RSV-CE)
"Fear not, for I am with you;
be not dismayed, for I am your God;
I will strengthen you, I will help you,
I will uphold you with my victorious right hand."

Psalm 56:3–4
"When I am afraid, I put my trust in you.
In God, whose word I praise,
in God I trust without a fear.
What can flesh do to me?"

John 14:27
"Peace I leave with you; my peace I give to you;
not as the world gives do I give to you.
Let not your hearts be troubled, neither let them be afraid."

Psalm 27:1
"The Lord is my light and my salvation; whom shall I fear?

The Lord is the stronghold of my life; of whom shall I be afraid?"
Joshua 1:9
"Be strong and of good courage; be not frightened,
neither be dismayed; for the Lord your God is with you wherever you go."

WHEN YOU FEEL ALONE

For the hours when loneliness presses close.

Deuteronomy 31:6
"Be strong and of good courage, do not fear or be in dread of them;
for it is the Lord your God who goes with you;
He will not fail you or forsake you."

Psalm 23:4
"Even though I walk through the valley of the shadow of death,
I fear no evil; for You are with me."

Isaiah 43:1–2
"Fear not, for I have redeemed you; I have called you by name, you are mine.
When you pass through the waters I will be with you;
and through the rivers, they shall not overwhelm you."

Psalm 139:7–10
"Where shall I go from Your Spirit?
Or where shall I flee from Your presence?
If I ascend to heaven, You are there!
If I make my bed in Sheol, You are there!"

Matthew 28:20
"And lo, I am with you always, to the close of the age."

WHEN YOUR BODY IS WEAK

For days when strength feels distant and fragility feels near.

Psalm 73:26
"My flesh and my heart may fail,
but God is the strength of my heart
and my portion forever."

Isaiah 40:29–31
"He gives power to the faint,
and to him who has no might He increases strength...
they who wait for the Lord shall renew their strength,
they shall mount up with wings like eagles."

2 Corinthians 12:9–10
"My grace is sufficient for you,
for My power is made perfect in weakness...
for when I am weak, then I am strong."

Psalm 121:1–2
"I lift up my eyes to the hills.
From whence does my help come?
My help comes from the Lord,
who made heaven and earth."

Psalm 18:1–2
"I love You, O Lord, my strength.
The Lord is my rock, and my fortress, and my deliverer."

WHEN HOPE FEELS THIN

For the moments when tomorrow feels uncertain.

Lamentations 3:22–23
"The steadfast love of the Lord never ceases,
His mercies never come to an end;
they are new every morning; great is Your faithfulness."

Romans 8:18

"I consider that the sufferings of this present time
are not worth comparing with the glory that is to be revealed to us."
Romans 15:13
"May the God of hope fill you with all joy and peace in believing,
so that by the power of the Holy Spirit you may abound in hope."
Hebrews 6:19
"We have this as a sure and steadfast anchor of the soul,
a hope that enters into the inner shrine behind the curtain."
Psalm 31:24
"Be strong, and let your heart take courage,
all you who wait for the Lord!"

WHEN GOD FEELS SILENT

For the hours when heaven seems quiet and prayers feel unanswered.
Psalm 42:5
"Why are you cast down, O my soul,
and why are you disquieted within me?
Hope in God; for I shall again praise Him,
my help and my God."
Psalm 13:1–2, 5
"How long, O Lord? Will You forget me forever?
How long will You hide Your face from me?
How long must I bear pain in my soul…?
But I have trusted in Your steadfast love."
Isaiah 55:8–9
"For My thoughts are not your thoughts,
neither are your ways My ways, says the Lord.
For as the heavens are higher than the earth,
so are My ways higher than your ways."
John 11:4

"This illness is not unto death; it is for the glory of God, so that the Son of God may be glorified through it."

Psalm 27:14

"Wait for the Lord;
be strong, and let your heart take courage;
yes, wait for the Lord."

WHEN THE NIGHT IS LONG

For the moments when darkness feels endless and rest feels far away.

Psalm 121:4–8

"He who keeps Israel will neither slumber nor sleep…
The Lord will keep you from all evil;
He will keep your life."

Psalm 63:6–8

"When I think of You upon my bed,
and meditate on You in the watches of the night;
for You have been my help,
and in the shadow of Your wings I sing for joy."

Psalm 4:8

"In peace I will both lie down and sleep;
for You alone, O Lord, make me dwell in safety."

Wisdom 3:1

"The souls of the righteous are in the hand of God,
and no torment will ever touch them."

Psalm 91:4–5

"He will cover you with His pinions,
and under His wings you will find refuge;
you will not fear the terror of the night."

WHEN YOU NEED TO REMEMBER GOD'S LOVE
For the moments when you fear you have been forgotten.

Romans 8:35–39
"Who shall separate us from the love of Christ?
Shall tribulation, or distress, or persecution…?
No, in all these things we are more than conquerors
through Him who loved us…
nothing in all creation will be able to separate us
from the love of God in Christ Jesus our Lord."

Zephaniah 3:17
"The Lord your God is in your midst,
a warrior who gives victory;
He will rejoice over you with gladness,
He will renew you in His love."

1 John 4:16–18
"So we know and believe the love God has for us.
God is love…
There is no fear in love, but perfect love casts out fear."

Psalm 136:1
"Give thanks to the Lord, for He is good,
for His steadfast love endures forever."

Jeremiah 31:3
"I have loved you with an everlasting love;
therefore I have continued My faithfulness to you."

APPENDIX C – STORIES OF HOPE FROM THE SAINTS

Stories of Physical Healing

St. Peregrine Laziosi

Peregrine Laziosi did not begin his life as a model of holiness. He was impulsive, quick-tempered, and part of a violent political movement in Italy. Yet grace often enters through the cracks of a troubled heart. After a dramatic encounter with St. Philip Benizi—a man Peregrine once struck in anger—he experienced a sudden conversion and eventually entered the Servite Order. Years later, as a priest known for compassion toward the poor, Peregrine developed a severe cancerous lesion on his leg. The tumour grew deep and painful, and the only medical solution was amputation. On the night before the surgery, overwhelmed by fear and sorrow, he dragged himself into the chapel and collapsed before a crucifix. He begged Christ to stay with him in the darkness of that hour. As he prayed, wounded and afraid, he fell into a deep exhaustion. In the quiet of the night, he saw Christ descend from the Cross and touch his diseased leg with tenderness.

When Peregrine awoke, the swelling had vanished. The next morning, the astonished physicians found no trace of cancer; the wound had closed, the tissue restored. From that moment forward, he became a sign of hope for the sick, especially those facing cancer. His life was not merely a story of miraculous healing but of God's mercy reaching into a heart that had once been far from Him. Through his suffering and healing, the Church learned anew that Christ still enters the places where pain feels most final and restores what seems beyond repair.

St. Charbel Makhlouf

Charbel Makhlouf lived hidden from the world, a quiet Maronite monk whose holiness remained largely unnoticed during his lifetime. He spent decades in silence, fasting, prayer, and service at the monastery of Annaya in Lebanon. Nothing about him suggested that he would become a vessel of healing for countless souls across generations. Yet God delights in working through the hidden, the humble, the small. After Charbel's death in 1898, an extraordinary light surrounded his tomb, and reports of healings began to spread. Many of these healings were of cancer patients—people whose bodies bore diagnoses that felt immovable. Stories came from every corner of the world: tumours disappearing without explanation, pain lifting overnight, medical scans shifting from despair to astonishment. The Church investigated, and the testimonies continued to multiply, not with theatrics but with quiet credibility, often verified by doctors who had no interest in exaggeration. Those healed consistently reported the same interior experience—a deep peace that rested upon them even before the physical change. Charbel's intercession became a window into God's tenderness. His miracles were never about spectacle; they were about the Father's love breaking through suffering to remind His children that He sees them, especially in their fear. Charbel's life teaches that holiness hidden in silence can become a fountain of hope for the broken, and that God is never limited by the boundaries of medical possibility.

St. Nektarios of Aegina

Nektarios, an Orthodox saint beloved by Catholics and Christians of every tradition, knew suffering intimately long before he became a healer in the eyes of the world. Misunderstood, slandered, removed from positions of leadership, he bore unjust accusations with humility and prayer. Later, as a simple monk on the island of Aegina, he became a gentle spiritual father to the poor, the sick, and the forgotten. After his death in 1920, God began to reveal the quiet sanctity that had marked his hidden life. Many cancer patients reported unexpected healing after praying for his intercession or being anointed with oil from his shrine. Nurses in Greece testified that when cloths touched to his relics were placed upon the bodies of the sick, tumours shrank, pain lifted, and peace descended upon those who had been tormented by fear. Scientific explanations were often lacking, but what remained undeniable was the transformation of countless lives through encounters with his intercession. Even more striking than the physical healings were the spiritual ones—patients who experienced profound interior calm, forgiveness, reconciliation with God, and the courage to face their illness with trust. Nektarios teaches that healing is never merely physical; it is the restoration of the whole person in the presence of God. His story stands as a living reminder that Christ continues to touch the wounded through His saints, especially those who have suffered themselves and learned the language of compassion.

St. André Bessette

André Bessette grew up frail, sickly, and uneducated—a man the world might easily have overlooked. When he was admitted to the Congregation of Holy Cross in Montreal, the brothers doubted he could contribute much. He was assigned the simplest duties: doorkeeper, porter, the man who welcomed visitors and swept the floors. Yet behind this humble façade lived a profound faith in the mercy of God and a tender devotion to St. Joseph. People soon noticed that those who asked Brother André for prayer often found healing—physical, emotional, spiritual. He never allowed attention to linger on himself; he simply pointed to God and to the quiet strength of St. Joseph. As crowds grew, André would anoint the sick with oil from a small lamp burning before a statue of Joseph, praying with calm confidence that God would do whatever was best for the suffering person. Cancer patients were among those who reported sudden improvement or full recovery, not because André promised miracles but because he trusted that God always listens to the cries of the afflicted. The physicians who witnessed these recoveries could not explain them, yet they were forced to acknowledge that something beyond human capacity was at work. André remained almost embarrassed by the attention. He insisted that the true miracle was faith itself—the courage to believe that God draws near to the broken-hearted. Before his death in 1937, he helped establish the great Oratory of St. Joseph, a sanctuary of healing and hope that continues to welcome millions. Even today, testimonies of healing flow from pilgrims who visit the Oratory or turn to André in prayer. His life teaches that God delights in using the smallest instruments to do the greatest works. The man who swept floors became a lighthouse for the sick, reminding the world that in the hands of God, humility becomes a medicine stronger than despair.

Blessed Luigi Novarese

Luigi Novarese's entire life was shaped by illness. As a nine-year-old boy in Italy, he was diagnosed with bone tuberculosis, a slow and agonizing condition that nearly killed him. His mother pleaded daily for the intercession of Mary, Help of Christians, and Luigi himself learned early that suffering does not silence heaven. Against all medical expectations, he recovered. That healing did not erase the memory of his pain; instead, it ignited a lifelong mission to draw close to the sick and wounded. As a priest, Luigi founded the Silent Workers of the Cross and the Marian Priests of the Sick, communities dedicated to serving the suffering and teaching them that their pain is not meaningless. He insisted that the chronically ill are not to be pitied from a distance but loved as people chosen by Christ to reveal His compassion to the world. Luigi witnessed extraordinary healings in his ministry, including cancer patients who experienced unexpected remission after receiving prayer and spiritual support. Yet he always emphasized something deeper than physical cure: the transformation of the heart. He taught that suffering offered with love becomes a fire that purifies the soul and radiates grace to others. The sick discovered through him that they were not burdens but bearers of light. When Luigi died in 1984, thousands testified that he had restored not only bodies but hope. His life stands as a testament to the truth that God heals in many ways—sometimes by changing the body, always by touching the heart and giving it strength to endure.

Stories of Spiritual Healing & Transformation

St. Thérèse of Lisieux

Thérèse Martin entered the Carmelite convent at fifteen with a heart full of love and a simple desire: to be God's little child. Her life unfolded quietly behind cloister walls, unseen by the world, marked not by grand missions but by small acts of trust. Yet her final months became a profound school of suffering. Tuberculosis ravaged her body, leaving her in constant pain, coughing blood, and struggling for breath. Doctors could do little to ease her agony. Still, within that fragility, Thérèse discovered a depth of faith that has become a beacon for millions. She wrote that suffering had taught her the meaning of Jesus' cry, "I thirst," and she longed to quench His thirst with love. What makes Thérèse's witness especially powerful for those facing cancer is the clarity with which she recognized that physical suffering does not erase dignity. Even when she felt her strength slipping away, she believed that God's love held her identity intact. Her "Little Way" emerged not from triumph but from weakness—the conviction that holiness consists in doing small things with great love, offering every pain, every breath, every fear to God. She once wrote, "I choose it all"—not because she sought suffering for its own sake, but because she trusted that nothing offered to Christ is wasted. Thérèse died at twenty-four, her face marked by exhaustion yet radiant with peace. Countless people who endure chronic illness or terminal diagnoses turn to her because she transforms suffering from a terrifying descent into a path of love. Her life reveals a truth central to every Christian story of sickness: when the body weakens, the soul is invited into a deeper intimacy with God, and even the smallest act of trust becomes a flame that lights the world.

St. John Paul II

Few modern saints carried suffering with as much transparency and courage as St. John Paul II. His life, already marked by early loss—his mother, brother, and father all died before he reached adulthood—became a long pilgrimage through weakness offered to God. As Pope, the world saw his strength: the athlete, the philosopher, the man who skied down mountains and celebrated Mass with the vigour of a young priest. Yet the world also witnessed his slow descent into physical fragility. First came the assassination attempt in 1981, then the gruelling recovery, then the diagnosis of Parkinson's disease, followed by numerous surgeries, tremors, and the steady weakening of his once-powerful voice. Physicians quietly reported that he battled cancer during those final years as well, though the Vatican did not publicize details. What mattered more than diagnoses was the way he bore them. John Paul did not hide his suffering; he allowed the Church to walk with him into it. Crowds saw his hands shake as he blessed them. They saw his body bend, his steps slow, his speech falter. Yet his eyes remained bright. He once preached that "suffering unleashes love," and he proved it by the way he embraced every weakness as an opportunity to draw closer to Christ. When asked why he remained so visible in his decline, he answered simply: "The world needs to see that even the frail can love." His final Good Friday, unable to join the Stations of the Cross outdoors, he followed them from his private chapel, clutching a crucifix in silence. The image of his weakened hand gripping the Cross became a sermon more powerful than words. For those living with cancer, his witness stands as a reminder that illness does not diminish dignity; it deepens it. John Paul taught the world that the human person reflects Christ most clearly not in success but in surrender, not in strength but in offering weakness as a gift of love.

St. Bernadette Soubirous

Bernadette Soubirous, the young visionary of Lourdes, knew sickness long before she became associated with miracles of healing. Poverty, asthma, cholera, malnutrition—her body was marked by fragility from childhood. After the apparitions, when crowds sought cures at the grotto, Bernadette quietly entered the Sisters of Charity, where hard labour and harsh conditions further damaged her health. Her knees swelled so painfully that walking became agony. Tuberculosis invaded her lungs and bones. Yet Bernadette never asked for healing for herself, even though she had seen the Blessed Mother and heard stories of miracles from the waters of Lourdes. When questioned about this, she replied with gentle humility: "My job is to be sick." She did not mean this in a spirit of resignation; she meant that her mission was to let God be glorified through her weakness. What is striking about Bernadette is not simply her endurance but her serenity. She lived what she called the "holy acceptance"—the belief that nothing is wasted when given to God. Her suffering became a hidden well of grace for others. Nurses and sisters testified that when they sat near her, they felt an unexplainable peace, as though suffering had carved out in her a deeper space for God's tenderness. On her deathbed, unable to move, she whispered repeatedly, "Holy Mary, Mother of God, pray for me, a poor sinner." She died at thirty-five. Decades later, when her body was exhumed, it was found incorrupt—an unexpected sign that a life offered in pain had become a vessel of glory. For cancer patients and all who suffer chronically, Bernadette reveals that healing is not only what God does to the body but what God does within the soul: the quiet transformation of fear into trust and of pain into a hidden form of love.

St. Gemma Galgani

Gemma Galgani lived a short life, yet her suffering unfolded like a long passion. Orphaned young, frail from childhood, plagued by spinal tuberculosis, migraines, fevers, and repeated internal infections, she carried a body that rarely granted her comfort. Yet her soul burned with love for Christ. Gemma experienced mystical graces—visions, ecstasies, and on certain occasions even the stigmata—yet her most powerful witness came not from extraordinary phenomena but from the way she embraced suffering with unwavering trust. When doctors attempted procedures to relieve her pain, she submitted calmly, even when treatments were primitive and excruciating. She once told her spiritual director, "If Jesus sends me suffering, I welcome it as a kiss." That was not naïve piety; it was the fruit of a deep conviction that Christ remains closest when the body is weakest. Gemma's final illness, believed by many historians to involve cancer affecting her respiratory and digestive systems, left her unable to eat, breathe easily, or rest without agony. Yet she prayed constantly for others: prisoners, sinners, souls far from God. Those who attended her bedside testified that she radiated a peace that had no earthly explanation. She died at twenty-five on Holy Saturday, her last words a whispered offering: "Jesus, You have my heart." After her death, countless people turned to her for intercession, especially those suffering with chronic or terminal illnesses. Reports of healing—physical and spiritual—followed, but her greatest gift remains the witness of her life: suffering transformed into a language of love. Gemma shows every wounded soul that pain does not have the final word; when united to Christ, it becomes a conduit of grace that touches the world in ways seen and unseen.

St. Elizabeth Ann Seton

Elizabeth Ann Seton's life was shaped by repeated encounters with loss, illness, and the fragility of those she loved most. Before becoming the first canonized saint born in the United States, she was a young wife and mother who watched suffering unfold around her with no promise of relief. Her husband, William, suffered from tuberculosis, and Elizabeth nursed him through long, painful months, bringing him to Italy in a desperate attempt to restore his health. Instead, she found herself widowed at twenty-nine, alone in a foreign country, grieving with five children depending on her. Yet it was in Italy, amid her deepest vulnerability, that she encountered the Catholic faith through the charity of friends. She was drawn in not by arguments but by the beauty of the Eucharist, discovering a God who enters human suffering rather than explaining it away. When she returned to America, poverty and illness shadowed her still. Two of her daughters died young; financial strain became constant; her own health deteriorated. Yet Elizabeth's suffering opened rather than closed her heart. She founded schools, cared for orphans, taught children, and formed the Sisters of Charity, a community that would serve the poor, the sick, and the dying for generations. What sets her apart for those living with cancer is her clear conviction that suffering never diminishes a person's identity. She wrote, "The accidents of life separate us from our dearest friends, but let us not be dismayed; God is nearer to us than they." Even when her body weakened, her faith only deepened. Doctors noted how pain left her exhausted, yet she pressed on with quiet strength, always returning to prayer. Her life teaches that suffering is not a barrier to holiness but the soil where trust grows. Elizabeth shows us that when life narrows through illness, the heart can widen in love, and that God's faithfulness remains constant even when loss seems relentless.

St. Peregrine

Though known primarily for his miraculous physical healing, Peregrine's life also reveals the deeper spiritual healing that unfolds through suffering—a healing many cancer patients experience even when the body does not recover. After his own cancer vanished through Christ's touch, Peregrine did not retreat into a comfortable life. He didn't wrap himself in the memory of a miracle. Instead, he became a companion to the dying, to the chronically ill, to those whose pain did not disappear. He understood something essential: physical healings are signs, not the whole story. The deeper miracle is the conversion of the heart—learning to trust God in every circumstance. Peregrine spent long nights in prayer with the sick, not promising cures but offering presence. Witnesses said that he carried a serenity that calmed the anxious and brought light into rooms otherwise filled with despair. Many were not physically healed, yet they died reconciled, at peace, ready to meet God without fear. Peregrine shows that the grace given in suffering is not measured by survival statistics but by the transformation of the soul—the healing of anger, fear, bitterness, unbelief. Those who pray through his intercession often testify not only to renewed health but to renewed hope. He invites every sufferer to discover that God's greatest healing does not always occur in the flesh but in the depths of the heart, where courage, forgiveness, and peace take root. Peregrine teaches that the miracle that matters most is the miracle that brings a soul closer to Christ.

Blessed Chiara Badano

Chiara Badano, a modern blessed born in 1971, offers one of the most radiant testimonies of hope in the face of terminal illness. At sixteen she was diagnosed with an aggressive form of bone cancer that caused unbearable pain. Her dreams—school, tennis, plans for the future—fell away one by one. Yet instead of withdrawing into despair, Chiara turned her suffering into an offering of love. "For You, Jesus—if You want it, I want it too," she would say each time the pain intensified. Friends who visited her expected silence and sadness; instead they found a girl who glowed with peace, who listened to their struggles, who comforted them even as her own body deteriorated. Nurses reported that her room felt different from every other room on the ward—as though light rested there in a way they could not explain. When doctors suggested treatments that might prolong her life but leave her unconscious or unable to speak, she refused. She wanted to remain awake, able to love to the very end. Chiara prepared for death not with fear but with anticipation, choosing her burial clothes—a wedding dress, symbolizing her readiness to meet Christ. She died at eighteen, whispering, "Goodbye. Be happy, because I am." Her life became a beacon for young people who fear illness and for anyone walking through cancer with questions that have no easy answers.

Chiara shows that suffering does not silence joy and that faith does not eliminate pain. Instead, faith transforms pain into a meeting place with God. She teaches that the human heart, even in its most fragile hour, can shine with a beauty that no illness—not even death—can extinguish.

APPENDIX D – ST. PEREGRINE
(Patron St. Of Cancer)

The story of St. Peregrine begins far from the peaceful images often associated with saints. He did not grow up gentle or devout. He was a young man swept into political anger and street violence, part of a climate in Italy where passions ran hot and crowds surged easily toward hatred. His heart was restless, wounded, unanchored. Yet God has a way of planting seeds of grace in the most unlikely soil, and the moment that changed his life came not in prayer but in the heat of conflict. During a confrontation with the Servite friars, he struck St. Philip Benizi in the face—a moment filled with fury, shame, and confusion. Philip responded not with retaliation but with silent compassion, and that expression pierced Peregrine more deeply than any rebuke could have. Something in him broke open. He felt himself seen for the first time, not as an enemy but as a soul worth loving. That glimpse of mercy became the hinge upon which his life slowly turned.

In time, Peregrine sought out the Servites himself, drawn to the peace he had glimpsed in Philip. The man who once raised his fist in anger now bent his knee in repentance, entering a community where silence, prayer, and service shaped each day. His conversion was not sudden brilliance but steady surrender. He embraced long hours of manual labour, penance, and ministry to the poor. He learned that holiness is found not in dramatic gestures but in a heart gradually softened by grace. Those who met him later in life described him as gentle, compassionate, and tender toward suffering. He lived Matthew 25 without realizing it—feeding the hungry, comforting the sick, seeing Christ in those who came to the monastery door. Years of service etched humility into his soul, yet beneath that humility was a quiet strength formed by sacrifice.

It was during these years that illness crept into his life, not as a small discomfort but as a growing, searing presence. A tumour formed on his leg, deep and aggressive. The pain increased until walking became torture, each step a reminder that the body has limits the heart cannot ignore. Physicians examined him with grave faces. The conclusion was unavoidable: the leg had to be amputated. Even in an age accustomed to suffering, amputation was terrifying, often fatal, and always disfiguring. Peregrine faced the diagnosis with the same humility he showed in every trial, yet fear pressed on him in the quiet hours. The thought of losing his leg felt like a stripping not only of flesh but of service—how could he care for the poor if he could no longer walk? Illness does not simply wound the body; it wounds identity, and Peregrine felt that wound deeply.

On the night before the surgery, he dragged himself to the chapel, his leg throbbing with every movement, his heart aching even more. He did not pray eloquently. He simply collapsed before the crucifix, sinking into a plea that rose from exhaustion rather than composure. He looked at Christ hanging broken and vulnerable, and he recognized his own fear in the face of his Savior. In that vulnerable moment, he asked for help—not with entitlement, not with certainty, but with the raw honesty of a man who had nothing left to offer except trust. The chapel was dim, silent, still. What happened next has been told and retold for centuries because it reveals something essential about God's tenderness toward the suffering. As Peregrine drifted into a heavy sleep, he saw Christ descend from the Cross and place His hand gently upon the cancerous leg. Christ did not speak. He did not instruct. He simply touched the place of pain, as though to say, "I am here."

When Peregrine awoke, the pain was gone. He looked at his leg and found the tumour vanished, the flesh restored as though no wound had ever existed. The astonished surgeons found no trace of disease, no need for amputation, no medical explanation. The miracle was immediate, complete, and quietly profound. It was not a spectacle for crowds. It was a gift offered in the stillness of a chapel to a man too weary to stand. Miracles are not proof that God prefers one person over another; they are signs that reveal God's nearness in ways we can touch and understand. Peregrine's healing was not a reward but a revelation: Christ does not turn away from human suffering—He steps into it.

When the Church later named Peregrine the patron saint of cancer patients, it was not simply because he had been healed of the disease. It was because he understood suffering from the inside. He knew what fear feels like when the diagnosis first arrives. He knew the helplessness of waiting for physicians to decide the next step. He knew the silent hours of dread, the loneliness, the questions that cannot be spoken aloud. His miracle did not erase the memory of that anguish; it sanctified it. He became a companion for the sick not as someone who had escaped suffering, but as someone who had walked through its shadowed valleys and found Christ waiting there.

The Church turns to Peregrine in prayer not out of superstition but out of communion. Scripture reveals again and again that the prayers of the righteous matter, not because saints possess power of their own but because they stand close to the heart of God. James writes, "The prayer of faith will save the sick, and the Lord will raise him up" (James 5:15). The saints participate in that prayer from the other side of death, interceding not as distant observers but as brothers and sisters bound to us in Christ. To seek Peregrine's intercession is simply to ask someone who understands suffering to kneel beside you before the Father.

For the one who carries cancer today, Peregrine's story is not a promise that every illness will vanish. Scripture never presents healing as a formula. Some are restored in this life; some are restored in eternity. What God guarantees is not a specific outcome but a specific presence. Peregrine teaches that Christ does not abandon those who cry out to Him in weakness. He shows that fear does not disqualify faith, that trembling prayer is still holy, and that God receives even the smallest plea offered in trust. Many people who pray through Peregrine experience physical healing; many others receive a deeper grace: courage for the journey, peace that steadies the heart, the strength to face uncertainty without being consumed by it. In every case, something within the soul shifts, as though Christ has touched not only the body but the places where fear lodges itself most deeply.

If you are praying for healing today—your own or someone you love—Peregrine stands beside you. He stands with those who wait for biopsy results, with those who sit in sterile treatment rooms, with those who lie awake at night pressing their hand against a place that hurts. His story is a reminder that God enters every space suffering tries to claim. Whether healing comes suddenly, gradually, or only in eternity, Christ never wastes a moment of your pain. Peregrine's miracle did not end with his restored leg; it continues in every person who discovers through his intercession that they are not alone.

And so we turn to him in prayer, asking not only for what the body needs but for what the heart longs for most—courage, peace, and the unshakable sense that we are carried.

Prayer to St. Peregrine

St. Peregrine, friend of the suffering and companion of the fearful,
you who knew the weight of illness and the terror of uncertainty,
stand beside me now as I place my life in God's hands.
Pray that Christ will touch the places where my body aches
and the places where my heart trembles.
Ask Him to give me strength for each day,
peace in every hour,
and trust that remains steady even when outcomes are unknown.
If it is God's will, may healing rise within me;
if He calls me to a longer road,
may I walk it with grace, patience, and courage.
Be near my loved ones as they carry this burden with me,
and teach us all to rest in the love of the Father
who never abandons His children.
St. Peregrine, pray for me.

APPENDIX D – FINAL PRAYER OF SURRENDER & TRUST

Lord Jesus, I come before You with a heart that is tired and a body that is fragile. Some days the weight of this journey feels heavier than I can carry, and my strength fades sooner than I expect. Yet even here, even now, I turn toward You. You know what fear feels like. You know the loneliness that settles into the night and the questions that rise without answers. You know the limits of this body You fashioned, the tremble of my thoughts, the ache that lingers beneath the surface. Nothing in me is hidden from You. Nothing in me is too small or too wounded for Your care.

I surrender to You the things I cannot control. I surrender the fear that tightens around my chest, the uncertainty that clouds my future, the fatigue that slows my steps. I surrender the days when courage falters and the nights when prayer feels distant. Hold everything I cannot hold. Carry everything I cannot carry. Breathe for me when my breath is thin. Be strength in the very places where I am weak. Teach me to trust Your presence even when I cannot feel it, to believe Your promise even when my heart trembles, to rest in Your love even when my thoughts are restless.

I place into Your hands the people I love—those who walk this road beside me, who worry silently, who carry their own fears for my sake. Protect them. Console them. Fill them with peace that does not depend on circumstances. Let my suffering never be wasted in their lives. Let it draw us into a deeper love, a steadier hope, a faith that rests more fully in You.

Lord, if it is Your will to bring healing to my body, I receive it with gratitude. If it is Your will that this cross remains for a time, give me the grace to bear it with trust. I do not ask for clarity—I ask for Your nearness. I do not ask for certainty—I ask for Your hand in mine. I do not ask to see the whole path—I ask only for the light I need for the next step. You have gone before me into every darkness. You remain with me in every moment. You will lead me through whatever lies ahead.

Take my fear and give me Your peace.

Take my pain and give me Your presence.

Take my weakness and give me Your grace.

Take my whole life, Lord, and make it Yours.

Into Your heart, I surrender everything.

Into Your wounds, I place all that hurts.

Into Your hands, I entrust my days, my nights, my hope, my healing, and my future.

Jesus, I trust in You.

About the Author

Matthew Sardon is a Catholic author from Melbourne, Australia, whose work is shaped by the depth and breadth of the Church's intellectual and spiritual tradition. Formed through extensive theological study within the University of Divinity and nourished by years immersed in both the Roman and Byzantine rites, he brings to his writing a unified Catholic vision rooted in Scripture, illuminated by the Fathers, and sustained by the Church's liturgical life.

His research and writing centre on biblical theology, patristic anthropology, and the mystery of theosis—how divine grace heals, elevates, and transfigures the human person. He is committed to making the Church's ancient wisdom accessible to the contemporary world, offering clarity and strength where many experience confusion and fragmentation.

Matthew is actively engaged in Catholic ministry, contributing to teaching, catechesis, adult formation, and parish mission. His work as a speaker and presenter reflects the same passion found in his writing: to awaken faith, deepen understanding, and help others encounter the transforming love of God.

You can connect with me on:
🌐 https://matthewsardon.com

www.ingramcontent.com/pod-product-compliance
Lightning Source LLC
Chambersburg PA
CBHW060104230426
43661CB00033B/1408/J